RATIONALITY, EDUCATION AND THE SOCIAL ORGANIZATION OF KNOWLEDGE

Papers for a reflexive sociology of education

Edited by
CHRIS JENKS
Department of Sociology
Goldsmiths' College
University of London

ROUTLEDGE DIRECT EDITIONS

ROUTLEDGE & KEGAN PAUL
London, Henley and Boston

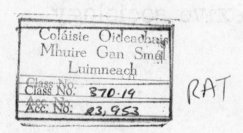
First published in 1977
by Routledge & Kegan Paul Ltd
39 Store Street,
London WC1E 7DD,
Broadway House,
Newtown Road,
Henley-on-Thames,
Oxon RG9 1EN and
9 Park Street,
Boston, Mass. 02108, USA
Reprinted in 1978
Printed in Great Britain
by Thomson Litho Ltd
© Routledge & Kegan Paul Ltd 1977

British Library cataloguing in Publication Data

Rationality, education and the social
organization of knowledge
1. Educational sociology
I. Jenks, Chris
301.5'6   LC 191

ISBN 0-7100-8513-3

CONTENTS

NOTES ON CONTRIBUTORS

PAUL FILMER lectures in sociology at Goldsmiths' College, University of London. He is co-author of 'New Directions in Sociological Theory' (Collier-Macmillan, 1972) and 'Problems of Reflexivity and Dialectics in Sociological Inquiry' (Routledge & Kegan Paul, 1975).

CHRIS JENKS lectures in sociology at Goldsmiths' College, University of London. He is co-editor of 'Worlds Apart - A Reader for a Sociology of Education' (Collier-Macmillan, 1976).

NELL KEDDIE until recently lectured in sociology at Goldsmiths' College, University of London. She is a contributor to 'Knowledge and Control - New Directions for the Sociology of Education' (Collier-Macmillan, 1971), editor of 'Tinker, Tailor ... The Myth of Cultural Deprivation' (Penguin, 1973), and co-editor of 'Worlds Apart - A Reader for a Sociology of Education' (Collier-Macmillan, 1976), she has also produced work for the Open University and published other papers in the sociology of education.

DAVID WALSH lectures in sociology at Goldsmiths' College, University of London. He is co-author of 'New Directions in Sociological Theory' (Collier-Macmillan, 1972).

MICHAEL F.D.YOUNG lectures in sociology at the Institute of Education, University of London. He is editor of and contributor to 'Knowledge and Control - New Directions for the Sociology of Education' (Collier-Macmillan, 1971); co-editor of 'Worlds Apart - A Reader for a Sociology of Education' (Collier-Macmillan, 1976); he has also published other papers in the sociology of education.

'When I came to men I found them sitting on an old conceit: the
conceit that they have long known what is good and evil for man.
All talk of virtue seemed an old and weary matter to man; and
whoever wanted to sleep well still talked of good and evil before
going to sleep.

I disturbed this sleepiness when I taught: what is good and
evil no one knows yet, unless it be he who creates. He, however,
creates man's goal and gives the earth its meaning and its
future. That anything at all is good and evil - that is his
creation.

And I bade them overthrow their old academic chairs and
wherever that old conceit had sat; I bade them laugh at their
great masters of virtue and saints and poets and world-redeemers.
I bade them laugh at their gloomy sages and at whoever had at any
time sat on the tree of life like a black scarecrow. I sat down
by their great tomb road among cadavers and vultures, and I
laughed at all their past and its rotting, decaying glory.'

Nietzsche, 'Thus Spoke Zarathustra'

Chapter 1

INTRODUCTION

Chris Jenks

Sociological enquiry characteristically takes as its starting point
some concrete conception of the nature and factual status of the
particular phenomenon that it is seeking to explain and account for.
This practice is in itself not remarkable as it would seem quite
usual to work from some initial perception of an object or activity,
constructed through the theorist's unique set of interests and concerns (or 'value orientations' to use Weber's terminology), and then
to proceed towards a more elaborated or 'disciplined' explanation.
What is important, however, is that the original premise of such a
process, the basic conception of the phenomenon that embodies and
symbolizes the theorist's particular grounds, is rarely made
explicit within the completed work. Through having been conducted
in this manner sociology is perpetually forgetful of that which provided for its construction and its meaningfulness. As a mode of
understanding sociology does not uncover or fails to display its
grounds. The fact that the individual theorist's grounds are not
made available for consideration within his work provides for the
possibility that sociologists, in the context of the practice of
their professional knowledge, can collectively address the social
world through an assumed or tacit consensus concerning the 'natural'
character of 'that' world. At the level of theoretic engagement
with 'the social world' there can be no real disagreement between
sociologists unless they specify their 'differences' by specifying
the various and competing grounds of their understandings. Let us
look, for example, at the reasoning behind a possible sociology of
education; the social practice being realized as interesting might
be made intelligible as the methodic transmission and acquisition of
systematically assembled bodies of knowledge by specific communities
of individuals in particular contexts. Such a conception as this
may be conventionally regarded as 'naming' the 'way things are', or
rather it may stand as instancing the covert agreement among sociologists, working within this substantive area, concerning the
factual categories which are assumed or taken-for-granted as existing in 'the social world'. By not being made explicit such taken-
for-granted factual categories (as grounded in particular interests)
are assumed to be representative of that very 'social world', and
thus, through tacit agreement, they take on the status of literal

descriptions. In the same manner that such assumptions provide for
the work of practitioners within the sociology of education, so also
do other 'agreed' substantive features of society make provision for
other sociological specialisms and for the overlap and boundaries
between them - we need only to look at the proliferation of sociologies of the family, religion, stratification, industry and so on.

What is consistently avoided, then, is an exposure or critical
address of the original conception of the 'social' and thus of a
particular phenomenon as itself social. Within such a tradition, at
its most simplistic or banal, 'society' may be regarded as assembled
from the totality of 'given' phenomena (the 'given' phenomena may be
more subtly rendered as the phenomena elected by the sociologist).
The structural concept of a totality of phenomena is suggestive of a
holistic approach to social theory, an approach which views a unity
comprised of interdependent parts. Such a view tends not to enter
into dispute with the factual preconstituted status of its 'sociological jigsaw'.

It would seem to be the case that as ordinary lay members of
society we all do exercise a practical interest in the real 'factic'
status of our world; It is the world of which we are a part and
within which we live, it is the world that we decide upon and in ac-
cordance with, and it is the world that we may seek to alter. As
such, the patterning of activities that we know as education is of
no conceptual difficulty to us. We may not claim to understand
fully the workings of the British education system, but as pupils,
as teachers, as members of an educated public we all 'know' what
education 'is'. This kind of everyday or 'natural' knowing is for
the sociologist the basic topic of interest. As sociologists we
must attempt to challenge the 'given' quality of the natural social
world and enquire instead 'How is such a world made possible?', 'How
is it constructed as such?'.

Questions of this order direct us to an appreciation of the
routine practices of members which afford for them an organized and
shared sense of the 'real', whether reality happens to be the social
experience of education or whatever.

In our sociological work we should attempt to reject the assumption that the individual as a social being has in some way been
placed into a society, that consists of a pre-established static set
of patterned relations, which he then comes to know by virtue of his
common membership, that is, through the process of socialization
into the collective heritage. Rather, we should pose as our
problematic concern the possibility that the individual, through the
on-going process of 'knowing' (or being-in-the-world), has constructed and continues to construct for himself in concert with
others, a 'sense' of his social existence and his social environment
as patterned and ordered. Thus, although as societal members,
questions like 'What is education?', 'What is rationality?', 'What
is knowledge?' may all present themselves as sensible and intelligible because they refer to features of our 'real' shared world, for
the sociologist qua sociologist they are inappropriate as they are
implicitly grounded in that reality as an assumption. The theoretic
task for the sociologist is not to make statements about the 'real'
forms of the world but rather to examine the meanings and the possibilities provided by these forms as constructed within a particular

social order. We need to ask, then, what is the 'form of life' or
common culture that can generate such questions and understand such
questions. The 'reality' that 'is' 'education', 'rationality', or
'knowledge' should not present itself as available to us as sociologists, we must regard it as 'strange' and we must look to account
for the socially contexted conditions within which such referents
(as constituting a lived-in-world) are meaningful.

The sociologies exemplified within this collection of papers,
though contexted as collectively constituting a sociology of education, might now also be regarded in terms of their more analytic
implications as sociologies addressing the methodic practices by
which societal members, and sociologists as members, come to produce
('know') education as an intelligible feature of their worlds. As
such they are what all sociologies might be - sociologies of
knowledge.

The problem of specifying the social character of our knowledge
provides the main shared orientation for our work gathered here.
Indeed, to pose such fundamental epistemological issues as 'How is
it that we know what we know?' and 'What is it that we are said to
possess when we say that we have knowledge?' is to address the basic
questions from which all forms of understanding proceed. For the
purposes of the sociologies that comprise this book, such questions
serve to direct attention towards the socially situated character of
'knowing' and further, to the context-bound nature of truth and
truth criteria as social rules of agreement. We can say that
'knowledge', like all forms of speech as action, is 'indexical',
that is, it is socially located in space and time, it emerges from
within a context and remains essentially inextricable from that
context - its meaningfulness and its truth value are situation specific. Knowledge then, like all social action, is intelligible as
contexted; its meaning is not trans-situational. Knowledge as a
'reality' stands as an 'index' of its located occurrence.

Clearly such a commitment to the concrete practice of knowing the
world as social produces the sociologies in this collection as
consciously critical of 'objectivist' theories of knowledge. This
criticism is made apparent in all of the papers through their re-
lentless address of the epistemological imperialism and legislative
oppression of Western scientific positivism - the dominant tradition
or 'logos' within which we all stand in our modern technico-bureau-
cratic world. Such a tradition variously views the social as
'naturally' ordered or preordained by some 'a priori' logic, and
thus it attempts, through the scientific method, to treat indexical
expressions as statements of objectivities.

Contained within this critical dialogue these papers articulate
two levels of consideration about knowledge. These levels are essentially linked yet nevertheless constitute two distinct areas of
discourse. The first level, which we may refer to as the
'concrete', involves here a concern for our chosen theme of education. It is apparent that all talk about education as a social
practice must necessarily rest upon some notion of what knowledge
is, however this may be explicated. To speak of the concrete, then,
is to speak of a commitment to the 'way things really are'. To
refer this to my earlier point concerning the acceptance of a
'given' world, largely such notions of knowledge are not explicated

and certain of these collected papers make reference to this
omission and attempt forms of retrieval from within the educational
writings of other theorists. The second level, which we may term
the 'analytic', entails a concern with our own activity as
theorists. These papers all display a common interest in articulat-
ing knowledge as a fundamental sociological problem of method. When
our work generates statements and accounts of the practices of other
societal members (concerning their view of knowledge or whatever),
those accounts themselves constitute a form of 'knowing' and are as
irredeemably indexical in character as are the shared understandings
of the people that we intend to explain. As Alan Blum puts it, 'Our
descriptions of indexical performance are indexically tied to the
conditions of their occurrence. Thus as a methodic activity our
work implies a conscious re-address of itself as an instance of a
tradition of knowledge, it requires that we should attend to the
social basis of our own mode of production. This is our analytic
task and it highlights our paramount shared concern, within these
papers, with the development and construction of a reflexive sociology. 'Reflexivity' speaks of the synonymous socio-cognitive
practices of interpreting the world and constructing the world as
interpretable. The theorist and his world, viewed through the meta-
phor of self-and-other, can now be viewed as analytically contingent
or rather essentially linked in the on-going dialectic of meaning-
giving and meaning-taking. Self-and-other points not simply to two
realms of being like subject/object, inside/outside, mind/society,
separate but linked by thought; rather it affirms the dialectical
process that provides for speech about difference and yet the experience of a totality (sameness), for example, to know oneself as
private and yet public, to know other as different yet reciprocal,
to know object as not-self yet needful of self's comprehension.
Reflexivity is that circularly interpretive problem of knowing a
'thing' and yet of providing for that thing as 'knowable' in that
way. Reflexivity might be seen as a feature of all understanding,
but in this, our sociology, it is elected as our specific methodic
topic.

From such a position, the writers of these papers consider education both as a concrete production of members in their worlds and
as necessarily an essentially reflexive feature of their own production. As theorists we here endeavour in part to see and explain
the practical accomplishment of societal members in constructing
their knowledge as an 'education' while ourselves doing or producing
an education as a form of construction. Such a reflexive irony as
this is always revealing, as is the irony implicit in the practice
of writing a 'persuasive' introduction to these papers - the a-
voidance of specifying reading instructions becomes itself an in-
struction about how to read them.

Nell Keddie's paper is concerned to demonstrate that whatever
activities or definitions might be held to represent education and
knowledge, they are no more (but no less) than the socially constructed outcomes of the practices of members in particular socio-
cultural contexts. Thus her work attempts to situate versions of
education specifically within versions of the social (as their
grounds). She examines the traditional approach of the sociology
of education which, she indicates, derives largely from a systems

theory perspective. Such a perspective renders education non-problematic and encapsulates deeply rooted assumptions concerning the distinction between 'concrete' and 'abstract' thought and a belief in an intrinsically superior Western scientific rationality. Nell Keddie further describes how such assumptions are promoted as basic judgmental criteria and are thus 'respected' as universally applicable to all accounts of other possible forms of education, rationality or thought. Through her use of the anthropological approaches of Garfinkel, Horton and particularly Gladwin, she quite clearly reveals the un-grounded and thus ethnocentric nature of the assumptions of the traditional work. Nell Keddie thus reinstates rationality and knowledge as concrete features of the practices of all societal members and as analytic troubles for all social theorists.

My own paper attempts to explicate the particular conceptions of knowledge and mind that provide the hidden grounds for certain dominant 'positive' forms of theorizing in education and in sociology also. The paper is occasioned by the writings of the eminent contemporary philosopher of education Paul F.Hirst, in particular his formulation of the logically articulated basic 'forms of knowledge' that he believes ought to self-evidently instruct curriculum planning in schools. For my purposes such epistemological structures and such policy instructions exemplify a mode of theorizing about ontologies that is potentially oppressive in its social consequences. My analysis aims at uncovering the systematic characteristics of such work, and by implementing the concepts of mind, knowledge and rationality it aims also at a demonstration of a method for a reflexive sociology of education.

The paper by David Walsh makes an explicit address of the supposed corpus of knowledge and sets of procedures that we commonsensically regard as 'the Sciences'. In so doing he is directly confronting the edifice that all of the contributors to this collection reject, namely, the tradition of positivism with its rule of phenomenalism and its implied correspondence theory of truth. He goes some way towards a demystification of the power of science by writing a sociology of scientific knowledge, an act partly inspired by the work of Thomas Kuhn. By conceptualizing science, and thus an education through science, as merely another method of appropriating the world, David Walsh indicates that science itself is a socially occasioned production rather than being the message bringer of an extra-social natural order. Such a formulation reflects critically upon the Durkheimian tradition of scientific sociology which ignores the issue that the social world, prior to being placed under the scrutiny of science, has already been appropriated culturally by the everyday practices of its members. A deeper analytic theme of this paper is that although scientific knowledge produces an 'efficient' method for handling and learning about the world it entails no way of handling itself as a phenomenon within that world.

Paul Filmer's paper offers an account of the importance of literary study as a form of liberal education within the works of F.R.Leavis, the literary critic. This theme is explored in terms of its implications for education and for a reflexive sociology. Paul Filmer investigates Leavis's notions of socio-literary thought and the development of a socio-cultural crisis, by using the concepts of the 'individual' and the 'social'. He then goes on to locate the potentiality for his sociology within a re-construction of Leavis's ideas of a 'common culture' and 'a language is a life'. Language is produced as the embodiment of a unifyingly human sense of community and as the crucial vehicle of any cultural tradition, both through education and as education. As such, language can be seen as the realization of our knowledge as a socially conceived corpus. Man's hope for authenticity and expression within the social are taken to reside within the reflexive act of 'collaborative creativity' contained in literary criticism and liberal education. Finally the paper affirms that sociologies, like literary works, are to be conceived of not as blueprints but as possibilities methodically grounded in versions of the social and thus antithetical to objectivists' 'ideals'.

In the last paper of this collection Michael Young focuses upon a typically assumed discrepancy between the realms of the 'theoretical' and the 'practical'. In this context the discrepancy is discussed in terms of the different perspectives held towards education by the sociologist of education and the teacher immediately involved in pedagogic activity. Their difference has important educational implications if it becomes established as a void of non-communication. Through a critical appraisal of different epistemologies and views on rationality Michael Young indicates the possibility of overcoming such a sterile separatist view of 'two worlds' - with one 'doing' and one 'reflecting' - and he works towards the constitution of a dialectically formulated notion of praxis with relation to education (or by implication any other feature of the world), which involves all people, as members of a common humanity, as active theorists. Michael Young's own grounds or tradition emerge through his dialogue with Merleau-Ponty's vision of knowledge as commitment - this secures all action as located within a specific socio-historical moment, and as such satisfactorily redeems the sociology of knowledge from the nihilistic prospects of a free-floating, 'anything goes' relativism. This paper serves also to illuminate the essential reflexive similarity between the practices of a sociologist in theorizing about a world as education, and the practices of a teacher in producing and changing education as a world.

The concern of all these papers is the construction of a reflexive sociology, their writers are thus compelled, through their chosen manner of enquiry, towards the constitution of a principled way of being-in-the-world manifested in and through their work. Having rejected invocations of a positivistic consensus ('what we all know') grasp of 'the' reality, we are committed to providing the analytic grounds from which we produce ourselves methodically as members and thus orient ourselves as theoretic beings in a negotiated meaning setting. By attempting to stand, at least analytically, outside of the tradition of positivism which for so long has been synonymous with the method 'sociology', we therefore dispute an absolute and final version of the real world as is conventionally assumed within such epistemological devices as the correspondence theory of truth, the sign-referrent theory of language and the transmission theory of meaning. Meaning construction and thus 'possible worlds' rather than 'final worlds' is our intent.

Ideas of the 'social' are thus taken to reside within members' conceptions or senses of the 'social'. Such conceptions in turn are not seen to be immaculately arrived at, rather they are treated as the outcomes of the 'work' of negotiation between members in community. This perpetually problematic process crucially involves the sociologist as member and as theorist; it is therefore his own form of rationality or tradition of method that is presented as the fundamental analytic trouble. Thus: 'How do we make sense of and thus elect phenomena in the ways that we variously do?', 'How do we construct worlds?', 'How do we produce a sense of the real?'

Reflexivity is the topic inevitably addressed in this work and is necessarily a constant feature of this work. Our writings attempt authenticity through making available the grounds of our understandings; as sociologists, as theorists, as members of a common humanity. It is partly in this context that our occasions and inspirations are drawn not only from established sociological traditions but also from contemporary philosophy, science, cognitive anthropology, literary criticism, teaching and so on; all are metaphors for possible societies or ways of being in the world.

The themes running through these papers have arisen through the contributors' shared concern with a sociology of knowledge and with a sociology 'as' knowledge. These interests have enabled us to dissolve the specialist categories of 'sociological theory' and the 'sociology of education' in our work both as writers and as teachers. As an outcome of this these papers are all 'theoretic' in the conventional sense that there exists no substantive centre-pin (except inevitably as a potential construction). The 'practice', 'reality', or 'essence' (if it may so be conceived) of the work is fought-for presence of a sociological way-of-seeing. To take an example, 'rationality' as a deep issue in social thought is explored here as it encapsulates and glosses over important questions about the nature of language, community and membership - vital concepts concerning all of our 'living' and 'living together'. Taken as a demonstration this 'introduction' might pose rationality as a problem for seeing this book as a collection, for seeing individual papers as instances of individual writers, for seeing a totality as an instance of the writer's collecting or the reader's collecting in-reading, that is, for seeing the 'rationale' for the book as a way of living or making sense.

To conclude and thus welcome you to the text, the papers that comprise this volume are all written by sociologists from within 'a' sociological yet human world. They have been gathered around the themes indicated in the title - Rationality, Education and the Social Organization of Knowledge. This exercise has been neither wholly intentional nor wholly arbitrary, like all knowledge it has been socially accomplished. The individual writers did not conceive of this work as a concerted and specific project in the manner of collections of writings around a particular concrete topic, in this sense the papers were written potentially but not purposefully in harness, they stand separately as explorations of theorizing a language of sociology. Despite the acclaimed absence of a substantive core, the social character or meaningful product that is this work emerges as unified through the writer's sense of community and through the reader's assembly and construction of such a community in his reading. This collection as a whole, like all collections and indeed like all understandings, may be taken as an instance of gathering procedures. The grounds for such procedures provide the 'being' of this book and are available to author and reader alike within the text.

'We come to know what it means to think when we ourselves try to think. If the attempt is to be successful, we must be ready to learn thinking.'

Heidegger, 'What is called Thinking'

Chapter 2

EDUCATION AS A SOCIAL CONSTRUCT

Nell Keddie

The initial critical focus of this paper is any statement which asserts 'Education is ...', since such an assertion precludes the
questions: 'What counts as education? For whom? Under what
circumstances?' That is, education is a problematic and socially
constructed category.

The systemic approach defines education normatively by treating
the educational system as a relatively unproblematic entity. Olive
Banks (1968) shows one way of setting this up (p.29):

The extent to which a modern industrial economy makes demands
upon the educational system is not in question. An advanced
technology can no longer depend upon the traditional 'on the job'
training. New and more complex skills require not only a liter-
ate work force but, in the higher echelons, a formal training in
science and technology. At the same time the concomitant ex-
pansion in trade and commerce gave rise to a demand for com-
mercial skills both at the practical and at the more theoretical
level. Finally, the education explosion itself, with its need
for more and more teachers, had a profound effect on the second-
ary and higher stages of the educational process.

We have encapsulated here a case that has been argued theoretically
not only by Parsons (1951) and also Glass (1954), Halsey, Floud and
Anderson (1961), Floud, Halsey and Martin (1956) and others in the
1950s and early 1960s, but also more recently in an apparently more
sophisticated form by Hopper (1968) and to some extent by Ioan
Davies (1971). Its basic tenets are:

1 There are necessary systemic relations between kinship, educational, occupational and economic systems which are sub-systems
of the social system and are held to exist theoretically and
substantively and by a process of boundary maintenance to account
for a sufficient degree of equilibrium within the social system as
a whole.

2 Stratification is a given or necessary feature of industrial
societies, in which occupations inherently require hierarchically
differentiated degrees of skills or talents (whose identification
is held as more or less self-evident but which are responsive to
change such as the recent redundancy of Latin as a universal university entrance requirement), and the education system responds

to this differentiation by feeding in talent at the right level of
the occupational system. This is, of course, one reason why a
commonly constructed index of educational success or failure is 'the
age of leaving school or length of schooling: it is an index whose
normative sense depends on a meritocratic concept of the 'occupational' system rather than upon an examination of the 'educational' system.

Dexter (1967) points out that, with a few exceptions (and these
might be held open to question), there is no necessary correlation
or correspondence between the activities that are assessed in school
and those skills that are needed for particular occupations. Why
should the ability to get five O levels fit you to be a nurse, for
example? The problem here is, can a taken-for-granted relation
between the two be articulated and made explicit, or might we not
find, contrary to Banks's assertion, that in many if not most occupations training is still 'on the job'? Few attempts have been made
to articulate and explicate the relationship that is generally taken
to be obvious (and in commonsense terms it may be obvious in so far
as it takes for granted criteria actually used by teachers and em-
ployers, but that is a different matter and poses different empirical questions from those that follow from normative statements).

Where attempts to clarify the linkage have been made they tend to
employ a notion of an abstract or 'rational' form of thought - with
its antonym 'concrete' thought - as central to the explanation.
This concept is employed by Bernstein (1971) in his paper, On the
Classification and Framing of Educational Knowledge, where he considers academic subjects in terms of 'deep structures' and meta-
languages, which is a development of his categorization of language
in terms of 'elaborated' and 'restricted' codes. It is also present
in the work of educational psychologists, not in any attempt by them
directly to relate academic to occupational skills, but in their
often tacit assumption that in school subjects inhere concepts that
can be ranked hierarchically along a continuum from 'concrete' to
'abstract' thought (for example, Bloom (1956), 'Taxonomy of Educational Objectives'). The child's mental development is conceptualized as developing along a similar continuum both by Piaget and
by the behaviourists. Piaget (1959) alone attempts to make the
links explicit. Fairly typical of its kind is Stones's (1966)
'Introduction to Educational Psychology', where the chapters on
cognitive development are not related in any way to the chapters on
school subjects. We may also note appropriately here the tendency
in all social sciences to treat what is termed 'cognitive' or
'rational' development as separate from emotional or 'affective' development, which is often tacitly assumed to be 'irrational', an
assumption that Garfinkel (1967) notes and undermines in his discussion of the way rational properties are attributed to commonsense
activities.

I shall discuss Gladwin's (1970) study of Puluwat Islanders in
'East is a Big Bird' to suggest that the whole distinction between
'abstract' and 'concrete' thought, together with the assumption also
made by Banks and others that literacy is a prerequisite or at least
a necessary correlate of 'abstract' thought, can be shown to be inherent in the way in which education has been defined by those who
make the distinction, and sets up to be solved problems that need
not be conceptualized as problems at all.

Before discussing Gladwin's data we need to examine a third tenet
present in the quotation above from Banks: that in considering education in industrial societies we have to take account of the
'needs' to be met by the social system in response to the rapid development of science and technology in the West. To get to the
central issue here, which leads eventually to the discussion of
'East is a Big Bird', it will be necessary to do some glossing of
what seem to be the common assumptions underlying this notion about
the 'needs' of industrial society in the sociological and educational literature. The glossing relies on the possibility (see for example, Kuhn (1970)) of seeing science as a normative activity and
holding in question the claims of the natural sciences to be by
definition positivist. These assumptions seem to be:
1 that rationality is distinguishable from irrationality;
2 that in Western scientific thought rationality exists in its
most quintessential form;
3 that industrialization and scientific progress are correlates;
4 that industrialized societies are distinguishable from non-
industrialized societies on various criteria (most of which, e.g.
urbanization, kinship organization, etc., are difficult to establish as empirically distinct within the supposed types of
social organization), of which rationality/irrationality is one;
5 that man in industrial societies is - or ought to be (the distinction is not always clearly made) - rational.
One quite explicit statement in educational writing which links
the evolution of rationality with the historical development of
Western science is to be found in R.S.Peters's contribution to the
Schools Council 'Working Paper No.12' (1967) (he argues the position
in more detail in 'Ethics and Education' (1966)), in which he le-
gitimates his argument by reference to Hobhouse, Ginsberg et al. who
claim the 'emergence of rational morality out of a great variety of
customary moralities and religiously sanctioned taboos'. Peters
argues (and his argument is strikingly similar to that of Parsons
about the unchanging nature of values at the highest level of generality):
Once the form of thought be it science or morality has developed
we should note that this seems to imply a cut-off point inhibit-
ing further development of the form of thought itself whatever
the changes at lower levels; a cut-off point which it would
prove hard to establish empirically , a certain kind of autonomy
and absoluteness goes with it. A man who thinks rationally in
these spheres cannot give up the law of non-contradiction and
many other principles which are pre-supposed in the general attempt to decide matters on the basis of reason. A rational man
can no more give up, in the moral sphere, the principle that he
should consider other people's interests than he can, in the
scientific sphere, give up the principle that he should decide
between alternative hypotheses in the light of observational evidence ... a degree of absoluteness at this level is compatible
with a vast amount of change and relativity at lower levels ...
The upshot of this is that when the question of relativity or of
changing moral standards is raised, people should be asked rather
sharply what level they are talking about. Are they suggesting
that fundamental principles such as fairness, freedom, consider-

ation for people's interests and respect for persons are 'relative' or in the process of being abandoned? Are they suggesting that the basic rules such as those relating to property, the
keeping of contracts, and the care of children are no longer
necessary or are in the process of being discarded? Or are they
preoccupied with detailed questions about sexual morality,
gambling, etc., which are obviously more contingent and de-
batable?

At the very least one may comment here:

1 that these 'fundamental principles' are treated as invariant
while we can only identify and experience them as socially situated and they are therefore contingent;

2 that, like Parsons, Peters attempts to account for historical
changes ahistorically; could he have made his comment about the
contingent nature of gambling and sexual morality in the
nineteenth century? Would they not have been treated as principles at the absolute level - to treat them as contingent contra-
dicts his own position.

In C.Wright Mills's (1939) terms, Peters fails to consider the
historically, socially constructed and situated nature (that is,
the 'relative' nature) of his own 'logic' or argument.

Peters argues that the essential and similar rationality of
science and morality stems from and relies upon principles of procedure which have a generality across the various spheres of rationality and have an absolute status. His argument here is laying the
foundation for the central interest of his paper which is normative
and political and appears later in the paper under the heading 'The
ideal of the democratic man'. The point worth discussion is not th
that Peters wants to discuss the relation between education and
democracy but that he sets the argument up in apolitical terms so
that issues of power are subsumed under an apparent discussion of
rationality and science. This strategy pervades much literature on
education; we may turn once more to Banks (1968, p.207) who, under
the heading 'Education and democracy', writes:

It may be appropriate to begin this section with a review of the
findings on the relation between education and democracy. It can
be shown that a discussion of the methodology by which these
'findings' were produced is a serious omission here, for example,
that the higher the education level of a country, the more likely
it is to be a democracy. Is Nazi Germany to be treated as an
unaccountable exception? Within countries, moreover, there is
an even stronger relationship between education and democratic
attitudes. In a summary of the main research findings, Lipset
('Political Man', 1960) argues that 'data gathered by public
opinion, research agencies which have questioned people in
different countries about their beliefs on tolerance for the opposition, their attitudes to ethnic or racial minorities, and
their feelings for multi-party as against one-party systems have
showed that the most important single factor differentiating
those giving democratic responses from others has been education.
The higher one's education the more likely one is to believe in
democratic values and support democratic practices. All the
relevant studies indicate that education is more significant than
either income or occupation. ... Particularly impressive in this

connection is Lipset's evidence that the working classes, and the less-educated, tend to be more authoritarian in their attitudes and to be more likely to favour extremist political and religious groups.

It is disturbing but common to find correlates treated as causal since the most obvious feature of this passage is its representative commonsense views about education pervasive among certain groups in our society which are also held to be self-evident by many sociologists. After all, the whole meritocratic consensus model (and in fact, often the conflict model too) of society rests on the notion that democracy/consensus/pluralism works because everyone agrees that those with most to give (merit and talent established by education) should have the highest rewards (status and income). This view is held as self-evident despite the concomitant view expressed in the above passage that only those at the top (those with most education and most to gain) really believe in tolerance and democratic values.

The second point about quoting this passage above is that the assumptions made there about education, industrialization and rationality impinge directly on the interpretation of life and thought in primitive societies which we shall discuss below.

The question of rationality, both as a special form of sociological enlightenment and as inherent in the sociological image of man, is examined by Garfinkel (1967, chapter 8) in a discussion that follows from Weber and Schutz and which encapsulates and tacitly points to the contradictions of Schutz's (1967) paper, The Problem of Rationality in the Social World. This is one of Garfinkel's most accessible writings and I shall point to aspects of it which are most germane to the focus of this paper. It opens:

> The programme of his discipline requires that the sociologist scientifically describe a world that includes as problematical, phenomena not only other person's actions but the other person's knowledge of the world. As a result, the sociologist cannot avoid some working decision about the various phenomena intended by the term rationality.
>
> Commonly, sociological researchers decide a definition of rationality by selecting one or more properties of scientific activity as it is ideally described and understood. The definition is then used methodologically to aid the researcher in deciding the realistic, pathological, prejudiced, delusional, mythical, ritual and similar features of everyday conduct and belief.
>
> But because sociologists find with such overwhelming frequency that effective, persistent and stable actions and social structures occur despite obvious discrepancies between the lay persons and the ideal scientist's knowledge and procedures, sociologists have found the rational properties that definitions discriminated empirically uninteresting. They have preferred instead to study the features and conditions of nonrationality in human conduct.

Garfinkel then inventories the various behaviours that have been designated rational in the literature, which 'may be used to construct an image of a person as a type of behaviour'; and he argues a distinction between those that can occur as part of the 'natural

attitude' and those that can only belong to 'scientific theorising'.
The latter involve attitudes that might well be repugnant in everyday life, like the calling into question of events that 'everyone
knows' to be the case. Garfinkel argues that 'the ideal characteristics that scientific observers subscribe to as the ideal standards
of their investigative and theorising conduct are used to construct
the model of the person who acts in a manner governed by these
ideals.' Von Neumann's game player, for example, is such a construction:

> Consider his characteristics. He never overlooks a message; he
> extracts from a message all the information it bears; he names
> things properly and in proper time; he never forgets; he stores
> and recalls without distortion; he never acts on principle but
> only on the basis of an assessment of a line of conduct for the
> maximising of the chances of achieving the effects he seeks ...
>   In a word, the model furnishes a way of stating the ways in
> which a person would act were he conceived to be acting as an
> ideal scientist. The question then follows: what accounts for
> the fact that actual persons do not match up, in fact rarely
> match up, even as scientists? In sum, the model of this rational
> man as a standard is used to furnish the basis of ironic compari-
> son; and from this one gets the familiar distinctions between
> rational, nonrational, irrational, and arational conduct.

Garfinkel recommends, of course, that:

> No necessity dictates that a definition of rational action be
> decided in order to conceive a field of observable events of
> conduct ... Instead of the properties of rationality being
> treated as a methodological principle for interpreting activity,
> they are to be treated as empirically problematical material.
> They would have the status only of data and would have to be ac-
> counted for in the same way the more familiar properties of
> conduct are accounted for.

What is of critical interest to us here is the way in which
Garfinkel points to the very central commitment of sociological
explanation to the notion of rationality, both as underpinning sociology as a scientific activity and in its notion of the ideal-
typical rational man, which in turn creates its correlates non-
rational, irrational and arational to characterize most human behaviour studied empirically.

Horton (1968), in the paper 'Neo-Tylorianism: Sound Sense or
Sinister Prejudice', takes up from within the world of anthropological debate similar issues to those raised by Garfinkel, about the
status and the nature of sociological or anthropological explanation. We may summarize his argument as follows. Because anthropologists have been so certain of the rationality of their own behaviour, they have seen the activities of members of so-called
primitive societies as irrational, arational and non-rational if
members' explanations of those activities are to be taken seriously.
When a member explains sickness in his family by reference to a
spirit world, his explanation taken at its face value can only be
called irrational and superstitious. The liberal academic anthropologist, because he takes for granted that Western scientific
explanation is more rational and therefore superior, becomes uneasy
about accepting members' explanations of their own behaviour at

face value because they are 'patently' nonsense. Therefore, the
members' accounts must be treated as if they were something else.
Thus, members' explanations given in terms of witchcraft are analys-
ed by anthropologists as if they were really explanations of social
power and then, the anthropologist argues, we can see that because
they are not what they seem to be, but really something else, the
savage is in reality a rational being since his social arrangements
exhibit features which the anthropologist can now 'recognize' as
'rational' (in that they now appear to serve some social purpose
recognizable to the anthropologist as reasonable and functional).
Horton writes (1968, p.626):

> The force of this contention is greatest in relation to the
> question of political manipulation. Modern social anthropolo-
> gists have been fascinated by the political manipulation of
> ·ideas - perhaps because it is one of the most obvious bridges
> between the Senior Common Room and the Assembly Place Under the
> Iroko Tree. However, their analysis of such manipulation has a
> curious unreality; and I think it can be shown that this unre-
> ality is the direct outcome of rushing in with a political analy-
> sis before having made an intellectual analysis.
> An extreme illustration of this point is provided by Edmund
> Leach's 'Political Systems of Highland Burma' (1954). Leach
> maintains that Kachin ideas about spirits are nothing but
> counters in the language of political argument; and it is pre-
> cisely this contention which convinces one that his analysis is
> unreal. One cannot help protesting that if the 'nats' are
> nothing more than counters in the power game, why do the Kachins
> waste so much time talking about them? Less extreme but more
> instructive is John Middleton's 'Lugbara Religion' (1960). Here
> is a book which starts with a vivid but rather conventional
> analysis of the way in which influential members of Lugbara com-
> munities manipulate ideas of ancestral power for political
> purposes and ends with what is perhaps the most brilliant intel-
> lectualist analysis of an African system of ideas yet made.
> Reading this book in the order in which it was written, one gets
> the same feeling of unreality as one had from Leach. Why do
> these people not get on with the politics? Rereading it with
> the intellectualist analysis put in before the political, one
> immediately regains a sense of reality. Now it becomes obvious
> why the old men spend such a lot of time talking about ancestral
> power and witchcraft when they are struggling for political
> position. It is because these ideas mean so much to the Lugbara
> as intellectual tools for making sense of the world that they
> are such powerful instruments in the hands of the politicians.
> If they meant nothing in intellectual terms they would be nothing
> in the hands of the politicians.

Horton argues, persuasively in the light of his own empirical work,
that this anthropological transformation of a member's explanations
need not be seen as liberal but as fascist, since by claiming to attribute rationality to him, it ethnocentrically prohibits the
member's explanation of phenomena being treated seriously at face
value. The anthropologist thus imposes meaning on his subjects'
ideas to take them seriously.
    In Horton's (1971) paper, 'African Traditional Thought and

Western Science', he shows how it has been customary for anthropologists to focus on the differences between African and Western thought to the detriment of the former. Horton shows that it is possible to point to the similarities rather than the differences and that, if you do this, the distinction between one as irrational and the other as rational becomes irrelevant: it can be seen as a false problem or as a 'trouble' of the anthropologists' 'own devising'. The point I want to make here does not have to do with whether or not Horton's interpretation of his data is to be judged 'true' or 'false', but to note that the way you set the problem up determines the kind of answer you get. To see Western science as a normative activity may lead to treating the explanations that members of other societies advance about the world with an equal respect.

To come now to Gladwin's (1970) 'East is a Big Bird', I hope it will be possible to argue that it can be cited as an empirical study which calls in question the whole complex of scientific rationality and cultural superiority and suggests - if the point is not already clear - that the distinctions drawn between industrial and pre-industrial societies lack the clarity and precision that would make them useful or enlightening. A correlate of this is that the distinctions between formal and informal education are also suspect since the notion of education as 'informal' (not institutionalized in a separate set of social organizations - schools, etc.) involves imposing a concept of 'education' on people who do not themselves use the concept and for whom it therefore lacks relevance.

In this sense, 'education' as a category is truly a relative social category and it is ironic to use a study of a people who do not use the category in its Western sense as a means of making this point. As we shall see, Gladwin is irremediably bound by his membership of a Western society to use the distinction between abstract and concrete thought to attempt to destroy the distinction. In fact, it is not really clear whether he is aware of how he has invalidated the distinction or whether he is attempting to reformulate it. This inconclusiveness may be because, like Horton (1968) and Goody and Watt (1962), he is troubled by what he sees as the problem of 'innovation' as a feature of Western but not of primitive cultures. I want to suggest that this is another 'false' problem of his 'own devising', though it may well be a problem for our common-sense notions of reality in terms of the perceived consequences of what we may term colonial activities, and would involve considerations about knowledge as power.

It is important to note what Gladwin takes to be his starting point problem not only to understand what he can give an account of but also to see what seems least satisfactory in that account. He presents his initial interest as the similarity between the poor lower class in the USA and illiterates or 'primitives' in their performance on IQ tests. He then raises many points raised by a critique of the concept of 'cultural deprivation'. In particular, he is interested in the nature of logical processes or cognitive abilities and strategies that the poor are able to bring to bear on the problems that are presented to them, rather than in the more usual practice of seeking to quantify divergencies from the psychological baseline used by educators. He is interested in other styles and

dimensions of thinking. He is fitted to undertake research among
the islanders of the Puluwat Atoll because he is an experienced
sailor and has had previous fieldwork experience among the Truk of
the western Pacific Ocean. In his study of the Truk he argues that
almost no useful work has been done (at least, by anthropologists)
on how people learn to think (or what is often termed 'cognitive
style') which he suggests is the correlate of the dominance of
Freudian constructs used by anthropologists (viz. e.g., Mead and
Wolfenstein (1964)) to explain 'socialization processes'.

I think one may argue that Gladwin is led astray, particularly in
the arguments of the last chapter of 'East is a Big Bird', in attempting to draw parallels between the cognitive style of the
Puluwat and the American lower-class poor. The fact that both do
badly on IQ tests does not justify his hypothesizing that the style
of Puluwat thought is akin to that of the American poor in significant ways. That is, he has not carried out a study of the cognitive
styles of the poor (a study which, incidentally, is sadly lacking
and long overdue). We shall return to this point since it is important for understanding why, in places, his account takes the
shape it does, particularly with reference to his notions about
heuristic devices or problem-solving procedures and innovation.

Turning to the ethnographic account we may note first that the
Puluwat can sail in canoes across wide stretches of sea (up to a
hundred miles) without sighting land and can steer accurately
without the aid of compasses and other instruments to landfall on
an island perhaps three miles in diameter. The following points are
of particular importance:
1 The first feature of navigation among the Puluwat is its pragmatic efficiency. It works, like sending rockets to the moon or
piloting a jet plane works. Predictability as a form of validation
is certainly one of its qualities.
2 Second, Gladwin argues, if navigation is viewed as a cognitive
system, then Puluwat navigation rests on a body of theory as well as
on specific techniques, and theory and practice (as in distance
estimation) are not always consistent. Some aspects of navigation
are also named and taught as distinct theoretically bounded systems,
for example star courses, wave systems and navigation when tacking.
Gladwin shows (importantly, if we wish to provide for the sense of
his account) that the Puluwat have no word for 'theory' or 'system'
but the subject areas specified are treated operationally (that is,
from our way of seeing) as of that order.
3 Gladwin insists that, while we can recognize and respect navigation as a pre-eminently intelligent activity, this is not its
significance for the Puluwat. It can provide a perspective on intelligence in our own culture, but the Truk do not view navigators
as intelligent; they view them as experts, as navigators.

Gladwin argues that Puluwat navigation theory is a theoretical
body of knowledge because it is explicitly taught and conceptualized
as a set of principles governing relationships between phenomena.
Phenomena are sometimes directly observed and at other times inferred - as the star compass bearing when the course star is not in
a position to be directly observed. These relationships are constructed from inferences and are unquestionably 'abstractions'.
Gladwin cites the Etak as an abstraction of a high order. The

concept of the Etak, of a specified but invisible island moving
under an often invisible navigation star (the canoe is conceptualized as unmoving and stationary), is not only an abstraction but also
a purposefully devised logical construct by use of which data inputs
(rate of movement, time passing, wave systems, etc.) can be process-
ed to yield a useful output: the proportion of the planned journey
completed. 'Abstract thinking' is therefore a pervasive quality of
Puluwat navigation.

Gladwin examines what he refers to as the abstract-concrete continuum in relation to such a concept as the Etak. A summary of his
argument illustrates how he is constrained by his own categories to
hold the opposite view to the one he is apparently arguing. He says
'abstract thinking' (at least, as it is conceptualized by educational psychology in the USA) deals with the properties of things that
are not usually obvious whatever that means, since the notion of
'obvious' here must raise questions about the nature of perception.
Often a quality must be inferred or its significance sought through
its being shared with other things which would not otherwise be seen
as related (procedures of categorization). 'Abstractions' range
from qualities such as colour or size (Conklin's (1955) paper on
Hanunoo colour categories illustrates very well how such categories
are socially constructed, situated and learned), which link objects
into classes to far more complex logical constructs embracing phenomena of several diverse orders (i.e. the concept depends on a
notion of prior categorizations which are more 'obvious') in complex
relationships. The Etak is a good example from Puluwat thought;
so, Gladwin says, is the work of the canoe-builder who in shaping
the hull uses knowledge (which incidentally he is not accustomed
to verbalizing) about the unobservable flow of water around the
lower parts of the hull. He is dealing with 'abstractions' about
forces and movements of water which he can only infer from surface
waves, sounds and the comparative performance of different hulls.
Then, says Gladwin, in contrast with such 'abstractions', 'concrete'
thinking is concerned entirely with immediately perceived qualities of an object or a situation. Once something has been observed, observation leads without further intellectual manipulation
toward one of very few possible responses. However, Puluwat
navigation is a system which simultaneously uses a 'fairly high
order of abstractions' and yet is 'pervaded by concrete thinking'
in, for example, the observation of wave systems which permit
individually a limited number of responses, but make sense within
the 'abstract' principles of the system.

What seems confused here is that Gladwin wants to retain the distinction between 'abstract' and 'concrete', since he has surely
shown that any so-called concrete thinking can be meaningful only
because of the abstractions or constructs that provide for its
sense: nothing can be simply 'directly observable' since some
construct must provide for the sense - which includes problems of
selective perception - of what is observed. Equally, the abstraction or construct only has meaning because it can be 'filled
in' or given sense within specific, 'concrete', socially located
situations. Otherwise they remain, in Garfinkel's words, 'ideal,
disembodied manuals of proper procedures'. One might comment here

that we have no studies on how the Western navigator practises
'proper procedure'.

Gladwin's study, it can thus be argued, can show us that:
1 rationality and the ability to make abstractions is not a
feature peculiar to scientific Western thought;
2 the distinction between 'abstract' and 'concrete' becomes redundant;
3 praxis is no guarantee of ontological status and validity.

Gladwin's study also illustrates another point made by Garfinkel:
that for researchers 'the difficulties in rationalising the concept
of abnormality' (or 'normality', for that matter) 'in the light of
cross-cultural materials may be troubles of their own devising'.
Gladwin is anxious to attribute to Puluwat and to lower-class American thinking a characteristic lack of heuristic devices. He claims
that neither are concerned with innovation and so neither think in
terms of trying to solve new problems. This is one of Gladwin's
most curious conclusions, for his data actually give the lie to the
hypothesis. Consider the following:

> Another of Hippour's presumably not unique spatial and angular
> sophistication followed upon my turning over to him, shortly
> before my departure, the chart of the islands we had both been
> using around Puluwat. This was laminated in flexible plastic for
> protection, and had the familiar circles which show the degrees
> of bearing and magnetic deviation. After taking the chart along
> on a trip to Pikelot, Hippour brought it back to me and inquired
> how to transfer a line of bearing between two islands on the
> chart to an adjacent bearing circle. He believed that if he
> could do this, even though he could not read the bearing numbers
> he could count divisions on the circle on the chart and thus
> transfer readings to his compass. Unfortunately in the last days
> before I left the United States I had been unable to purchase the
> parallel rulers which are customarily used for this purpose and
> instead had brought along an adjustable protractor. The pro-
> tractor was especially inconvenient because it moved only through
> a 45-degree span and had to be turned round to complete the 90-
> degree sector. All in all the process was so complicated and
> confusing that I put it aside for use only if in an emergency I
> had to navigate myself. No such emergency arose and I forgot it.
> So I got out the protractor and did my best to explain it to
> Hippour. To my amazement he soon said he understood, and showed
> me by applying the device a couple of times in ways that seemed
> appropriate. I was not on the island long enough thereafter to
> follow up and determine if he had really mastered the protractor,
> but he was at least enthusiastic and delighted to have it.
> (Gladwin, 1970, p.142)

Why is it that, in the light of a passage like that, Gladwin can
argue that Puluwat thought lacks heuristic devices and as an ex-
tension of that claim that the American poor also lack these strategies, although his work has made no direct study of them? It seems
that he is bound by two assumptions that he has left unquestioned:
1 What is to count as a problem-solving strategy: the kind of
heuristic device demanded by IQ tests in particular and probably by
most schooling in general in the West demands mastering strategies

that are frequently alien to the 'real-life' problems that people
need to solve. To treat all problem-solving activities as if they
were of the same order, independent of the social context in which
they have significance, is to work with a very limited notion of
heuristics.

   2 Despite the main tenor of his work he is hampered by a more
  general notion of what counts as 'innovation' which hinges on the
sociological/anthropological dichotomy between industrial and pre-
industrial societies. These distinctions notoriously resist empirical reification under such headings as 'urbanization', 'the family',
etc., but the general presumption seems to be that in the West
thought and material progress have been evolutionary and cumulative
(however, see Kuhn (1970) and D.Walsh's paper in this book), while
'primitive' societies remain 'static' (despite increasing evidence
to the contrary) and in a state which Durkheim describes as 'mechanical solidarity', in which the 'conscience collective' makes
innovation impossible. This is of particular interest in the
context of educational discussion, since working-class children are
described as exhibiting all the characteristics of people living in
a state of mechanical solidarity. The question that is seldom
raised, since it is evaded by the taking of social class for
granted, is how such people have managed to survive for so long and
in such numbers in an industrialized society which by definition
(see Parsons (1951)) exhibits necessarily the features of organic
solidarity and individualism.

   It is the strength of Gladwin's study that he can focus for us
questions like this although he himself fails to take them seriously. His conclusions seem to remain 'troubles of his own devising',
but the following passage, which serves as a fitting close, shows
how aware he is of the problem of 'anthropological strangeness' and
the degree to which he is aware that it is necessary and yet irremediably impossible to give an anthropological gloss of how he ac-
quired member's knowledge among the Puluwat. A sociologist seeking
the same sort of knowledge of the poor in our society must face the
same problems.

   Like everything else in this chapter the words which follow are
   mine. Although Hippour and other navigators refer explicitly to
   a moving island when talking about etak or tacking, the larger
   logical context in which this concept operates is not described
   by them in words. This does not mean it is not real to them; it
   means only that they share and take for granted all cognitive
   antecedents of saying that an island 'moves'. They find no need
   and therefore have no practice in explaining this to someone like
   myself who starts out thinking of the voyage as a process in
   which everything is fixed except the voyagers. The situation I
   suspect would be similar if an American, accomplished in interpreting the stylised symbols and distortions of a highway map,
   were asked to explain to our old friend the man from Mars what he
   really means when he points to the map and says 'We are here'. I
   arrived, through my own style of induction, at a description of
   the Puluwat navigator's cognitive map, the only description I
   could conjure up which would account for all the different things
   that a number of different people said in the course of trying to
   me what etak was all about (tacking came later). Having arrived

at this construct I explained it carefully to Hippour, as was my custom whenever I felt I had mastered a particular topic. He agreed in broad outline but made one modification, one which in itself encouraged me to believe he understood what I was saying. Later in talking with other people, and in particular when it came time for me to learn about navigation when tacking, I found my perception of the system could be used without leading to any more misunderstandings. In other words it made sense out of everything that followed, both familiar and new. It is for this reason in particular that I am satisfied the cognitive map I constructed is real. That is, real in the sense that I correctly understood how the navigators organised their information. I would certainly not suggest they believe islands actually move any more than the man with his finger on the road map believes he is really somewhere in the spot of ink on the paper. (Gladwin, 1970, pp.181-2)

BIBLIOGRAPHY

BANKS, O. (1968), 'The Sociology of Education', Batsford.
BERNSTEIN, B. (1971), On the Classification and Framing of Educational Knowledge, in M.F.D.Young (ed.), 'Knowledge and Control', Collier-Macmillan.
BLOOM, B.S. (1956), 'Taxonomy of Educational Objectives', New York, David McKay.
CONKLIN, H. (1955), Hanunoo Color Categories, 'Southwestern Journal of Anthropology', vol.11, Winter.
DAVIES, I. (1971), The Management of Knowledge: a Critique of the Use of Typologies in the Sociology of Education, in M.F.D.Young, 'Knowledge and Control', Collier-Macmillan.
DEXTER, L. (1967), On the Politics and Sociology of Stupidity, in H.Becker (ed.), 'The Other Side', New York, Free Press.
FLOUD, J.E., HALSEY, A.H. and MARTIN, F.M. (1956), 'Social Class and Educational Opportunity', Heinemann.
GARFINKEL, H. (1967), 'Studies in Ethnomethodology', Englewood Cliffs, N.J., Prentice-Hall.
GLADWIN, T. (1970), 'East is a Big Bird', Cambridge, Mass., Harvard University Press.
GLASS, D.V. (1954), 'Social Mobility in Britain', Routledge & Kegan Paul.
GOODY, J. and WATT, I. (1962), The Consequences of Literacy, 'Comparative Studies in History and Society', vol.5, no.3.
HALSEY, A.H., FLOUD, J. and ANDERSON, C.A. (1961), 'Education, Economy and Society', New York, Free Press.
HOPPER, E. (1968), A Typology for the Classification of Educational Systems, 'Sociology', vol.2, no.1.
HORTON, R. (1968), Neo-Tylorianism: Sound Sense or Sinister Prejudice, 'Man' (n.s.), vol.3.
HORTON, R. (1971), African Traditional Thought and Western Science, in M.F.D.Young, 'Knowledge and Control', Collier-Macmillan.
KUHN, T. (1970), 'The Structure of Scientific Revolutions', University of Chicago Press.
LEACH, Edmund (1954), 'Political Systems of Highland Burma', Bell.

MEAD, M. and WOLFENSTEIN, M. (1964), 'Childhood in Contemporary Cultures', University of Chicago Press.
MIDDLETON, John (1960), 'Lugbara Religion', International African Institute.
MILLS, C.Wright (1939), Language, Logic and Culture, 'American Sociological Review', vol.4, no.5.
PARSONS, T. (1951), 'The Social System', Routledge & Kegan Paul.
PETERS, R.S. (1966), 'Ethics and Education', Allen & Unwin.
PETERS, R.S. (1967), The Status of Social Principles and Objectives in a Changing Society, in 'Schools Council Working Paper', no.12.
PIAGET, J. (1959), 'Language and Thought of the Child', Routledge & Kegan Paul.
SCHUTZ, A. (1967), The Problem of Rationality in the Social World, in 'Collected Papers', vol.II, The Hague, Martinus Nijhoff.
STONES, E. (1966), 'Introduction to Educational Psychology', Methuen.

Chapter 3

POWERS OF KNOWLEDGE AND FORMS OF THE MIND

Chris Jenks

It is increasingly the case that sociologies concerned with education as a field of practical accomplishment are beginning to treat
seriously the problems involved in man's various conceptions of the
nature of knowledge. It has been described by Young (1971) that the
tradition provided by the sociology-of-education has largely ignored
or glossed over such considerations implicitly, it may be imputed,
on the basis that 'knowledge' constitutes the bedrock or 'very
stuff' of education and is in that sense 'given' and not available
for analysis. Such an approach has therefore tacitly assumed the
grounds for the argument to be developed here, and indeed the
grounds of its own renderings.

The intention of this paper involves an attempt to invite the
reader as theorist to reawaken, restate or reconstruct the themes of
the nature of 'mind' and 'knowledge' as being essential features of
our discourse (within any sociology of education). These themes of
the nature of 'mind' and 'knowledge' I take to be fundamental to all
talk about education, and I therefore suggest that previous work, by
eschewing such considerations as perhaps beyond the province of
sociological inquiry, has in the main restricted its energies to re-
hearsals of what are by now institutionalized, and what appear
basically to be positivistically formulated epiphenomena. Traditional explorations of such problems as ability, differential
achievement, educational opportunity, socialization, teaching-learn-
ing and curriculum planning all rest necessarily on strong but unexplicated theories of the nature of mind and knowledge - we must
look to their grounds.

It is interesting to note that within theories concerning education such questions addressing mind and knowledge have fallen
under the aegis of the philosophers (as specialists) - I wish to
claim them back! The method of this paper then is to approach the
question of the corpus of educational knowledge as it has come to be
formulated within the activity seen as the philosophy of education,
and to attempt to provide for a sense of what may be treated as this
dominant account of the 'forms of knowledge' as articulated more
generally within the language of educators.

The specific occasion for this paper is the work of the philosopher Paul H. Hirst; by critically providing for his intelligibility

I shall attempt to recover a sense of my own theorizing. This is necessarily located within my rendering or reading of Hirst's position which occurs as the text.

It must be emphasized that throughout, all notions of forms or categories of knowledge are taken to be constructed as features of the philosopher's method; that is, they are statements of the form of life of the theorist; they express his selected method of analysis. In the same way, my reading of Hirst's position is a feature of my method and the reader's construction of my argument is a feature of his method. It may be seen then that the truly analytic character of such an enterprise resides in the theorist's form of life, his method of doing categorization - that which is to be disclosed. As theorist then, I am not aiming at anonymity; my purpose is not to critically review an 'out-there' slice of posited reality; I am in the business of categorization and construction; I am committed to showing the character of my own reasoning.

It should therefore be available from my approach that a sociological concern with the problems that are knowledge applies essentially to our own individual knowledge (that is, our-Selfs as knowledge) while making considerations of any versions of knowledge other than ourselves. In the context of this form of theorizing references to Self and knowledge (theorist and tradition) are not intended to imply self as a concrete biographical identity. To talk of a Self as theorist is to talk of Self as belonging to a tradition (commitment to a way of formulating). (1) Thus my endeavour in expressing the philosopher's method or tradition (of knowledge and as knowledge) is to produce a Self-explicating course of writing - I attempt to display my sociological tradition. In so doing I attempt to show my view of 'knowledge' and 'mind' as displays of my knowledge and mind. Similarly, all members as theorists (as belonging to traditions) fashion their worlds as knowledge.

These remarks are meant to convey a dominant concern with the ongoing problem of reflexivity. The reflexive nature of understanding may be initially stated as the methods by which a member seeks to account for and make sense of the appearances of his world are the methods by which he provides for that world of appearances; so that the processes by which we produce accounts of the world are productions of that world as that world.

My method then requires that we treat knowledge in terms of accounting procedures - that is, as being of a social world and therefore amenable to negotiated social rules in community. When considering knowledge it is not a posited essence or intrinsic entity that I seek to describe, but rather perhaps the management of explanation such that knowledge is seen to be displayed in a social context. Thus, the question shifts from a notion of 'What is knowledge?' to the question of 'How does knowledge get done?' What, we need to ask, is the nature of the epistemic community in which knowledge as 'proper knowledge' can be seen to be appropriately displayed? It is only by addressing the sociological question of the possible nature of the community that we can attempt to grasp analytically what it is that makes 'knowledge' recognizable as such. Our question is then 'Wherein resides the recognizability of knowledge?'

At a substantive level then schools would need to be conceptual-

ized as arenas where teachers and pupils (as members) interact in a
process of negotiating the assessment of the children's display of
appropriate knowledge. Knowledge could not be seen as an entity
that is constant, that can be realized in a one-to-one meaning-
naming manner, and be thus amenable to objective quantification.
We might note that the sociology-of-education has traditionally
always directed its attention to within the context of schools or
similar 'formal educational' establishments as being somewhere where
knowledge is always seen to reside; it is as if all other possible
forms of community operated without knowledge or were incapable of
generating knowledge.

   It is positivism as the conventional epistemology that has generated the obsessional analytic stance dominated by a correspondence
theory of truth - it is this thought style that orients the
practices of education, science, sociology and indeed most Western
intellectual endeavour. As McHugh (1970) has pointed out, positivism operates with 'a sheer asocial logic' in that knowledge as truth
is treated as necessarily a feature of the private understandings of
individuals as any-man. Knowledge is taken as a constant universe
of truth available as the World, to which an individual incorporat-
ing the mechanism that is mind has pure unobstructed access as
correspondence. As long as the individual employs the 'correct'
method (which produces him as any-man) his perceptions will correspond with the 'out-there', reality structure. (2) Knowledge as
truth is therefore seen to be realized as a feature of individual
competence; this is a stance that wholly denies the possibility of
the social grammar of performance. Membership, shared or negotiated
understandings and ultimately communication are denied - except perhaps in terms of a community of same-truth speakers. As sociologists, our practices are essentially directed to the explication
and understanding of the social grammar of performance; that is,
the methodic procedures by which we generate a sense of community
and of knowledge, and indeed by which we generate a sense of the
social.

   This brings me initially to the question of conceptions of the
nature of mind. Perhaps the most popularly held view of mind and
of the development of mind (as education) is a version of the empiricist or naturalistic position. Such a conception is individual-
istic; it holds either that mind is spatialized like an empty
vessel awaiting to be filled - a vacuum that both nature as material
reality and education its handmaiden abhors, or that mind is equip-
ped with an individually located but universally conceived mechanism
(the 'ghost' in the machine). The space or the mechanism are then
fed through experience, that is via the constant neutral agencies
that are the senses, by the vast constellation of information that
constitutes the universe. In this way mind qua mind develops,
understandings are generated and the individual enters into the
shared world of reality; shared, that is, by minds qualitatively
similar but various in accord with their own particular sensual bi-
ography and level of physiological development. The business of
education is thus defined as providing a positive and uniform vocabulary of experiences to be impressed upon developing minds.
Teaching thus becomes active implantation or mind-sculpting, and
learning becomes the passive contemplation and imitation of ob-

jective structures. Educational failure (that is learner's failure
as perceived) can thus be understood in terms of a form of deprivation (of experience) or perhaps in terms of the different capaci-
ties or efficiencies of the individual learners' machines. Talk of
'bad backgrounds' or 'working within limitations' reflects a tacit
acceptance of this view. (3)

In the context of my own set of elections, such a view of mind is
concrete and mechanistic; it glosses over important questions about
the nature of perception; it fails to treat seriously the individual as a Self and theorist, and once again it dispenses with language
as the social context of meaning.

It is interesting here to note the work of Freire (1970,1972) on
adult literacy programmes which he sees as sinister political imple-
ments of control. He describes their conception of the literacy
process as 'mechanistic' or displaying a 'naive technicality', and
suggests that such programmes have an underlying 'naturalistic' view
of man - illiterates are seen as having undernourished consciousnesses which have to be filled or fed; they are taken as passive
beings, as object of the process of learning to read and write, not
as its subject.

In the context of this paper Freire provides us with a critique
of the view of mind underlying such programmes and the consequences
of such a conception. He suggests that such programmes reveal a
failure to perceive not only the structure of literacy, but the
structure of social phenomena in general - that is, their individu-
alistic competence-based orientation ignores the socially occasioned
production of learning and knowledge. (4)

Freire's radical directive which resonates with a major sense of
this paper is that: 'Illiterates are not "beings-outside-of" they
are "beings-for-another". Their solution is not to become "beings-
inside-of" but men freeing themselves - in reality they are not men
marginal to the structure but rather men oppressed in it. They
cannot become incorporated, they must authentically transform the
dehumanizing structure.'

His policy implications point to a political notion of praxis, of
authentic dialogue between the teacher and the taught, of the
learner assuming an awareness of his right and capacity as a human
to transform the world. Learners therefore must be creative
subjects; the human word for Freire 'is more than mere vocabulary -
it is word-in-action'; and speaking the word is a 'human act imply-
ing reflection and action'. (5)

For our purposes, Freire is speaking to the sense of the Self as
practical theorist, and of knowledge not as an objective structure
requiring inductive procedures but rather as the negotiated tradition of discourse within social settings.

The empiricist view of mind has received treatment by both Ryle
(1949) and Wittgenstein (1953). Ryle's work can be read as stating
that to treat mind as a ghost embodied in a machine is to operate
with a form of discourse that is applicable to the order of things
or objects, but which is not necessarily applicable to talk about
minds. To talk about mind is not to talk about a list of objective
or material attributes; it is rather to talk about an individual's
socially conceived ability to carry out certain kinds of performance. Thus to speak of mind as 'knowing' is to speak about par-

ticular types of action indicating that 'knowing' has or is being
done - the knowing is located in the social world of performance,
not in the private and impenetrable world of 'the ghost'

Seeing Wittgenstein through his guiding statement of 'the meaning
of a word is its use in the language', it is available that he is
commenting on the nature of mind in his remarks on 'inner states'.

Now Wittgenstein's concern with the 'use' context of language
(and the problem of reflexivity) places him in opposition to views
belonging to the meaning-naming theory of language (see his
'Tractatus') or to views that consider the meaning of a word to be
whatever the speaker has in mind or feels 'privately'.

Just as any talk about games does not label an essential nature
of 'the game', so any talk about 'pain' or 'sensations' (Wittgenstein's examples) does not reflect or label an essential nature of
'pain' or 'sensations'. Thus there is inevitably no essential
nature of 'sensations'; it makes no sense to say that 'sensations
are private', and thus it makes no sense to say that 'meanings are
private'.

'Meanings' like 'sensations' are available to us only within the
conventions of a language game. They are public or they are
meaningless. If you cannot tell me about them then how or where can
they possibly reside; if you can tell me about them then they are
not private. To say that 'sensations are private' and to be understood trades upon our knowledge of sensations-in-use. (6)

In Wittgenstein's terms to talk about 'private sensations' is to
confuse the grammar or systematic use of the word 'sensation' with
a form of discourse concerning the 'factual' realm of non-linguistic
entities. So all meanings like all sensations are ways of life made
possible by the use of language - mind is only available by the use
of language.

When we consider various 'inner states' of mind, when we consider
the criteria of these states we disclose the uses of various expressions - or by noticing the uses of various expressions we come
to acknowledge what patterns of action provide for our use of these
terms. Finally then, we can assert that reference to 'inner states'
is redundant, we require only reference to a series of grammars. In
the same manner that we have a language of pleasure or of pain we
have also languages of memory, inspiration, understanding, recognition. To understand the nature of some possible feature of our
world (like mind) is to understand the language (as grounds) that
gave rise to the questions concerning it as a possibility.

Empiricist views of mind or of the development of mind face the
constant problem of sociological positivism, that is of how to get
the 'outside' on to the 'inside' - of how to internalize the external (the real object world). Such problems are traditionally
subsumed under theorizing about socialization.

We may now begin a treatment of Hirst's work. For our purposes
Hirst's writing on the 'forms of knowledge' is important in that it
serves to assemble what I have elected as important analytic issues,
namely the nature of mind and knowledge, within the context of educational discourse. Further, it constitutes a paradigm case of
certain ways of proceeding (his form of theorizing) to which I am in
opposition. Hirst then constitutes an almost isolated gathering of
the fundamental themes that I wish to critically address - it is

hoped that my unravelling of his position will provide a way to my
way of seeing.

Concretely, Hirst's work invites treatment because of its established formidable character - that is, it is extremely influ-
ential in teacher training courses generally, and also within work
on curriculum planning (like that of the Schools Council). The work
has standing; it is deemed acceptable; and like too much in the
field of 'educational theory' it tends to be read as a final
statement - as such its use forecloses the kind of reconstruction
recommended here.

Hirst (1965) sets out from a practical concern with the es-
tablishing of a 'positive' definition of the concept 'liberal education' (a concept of which he approves despite its apparent
elusiveness) as a potential guiding structure for educational planning. His working model for analysis becomes an 'education based
fairly and squarely on the nature of knowledge' His philosophical
task thus becomes one of informing us on the 'nature of knowledge';
what he must necessarily be telling us however is his version of the
'true' nature of knowledge - otherwise the justifications provided
for one more relative definition of a set of practices and axioms
called liberal education could claim no legislative superiority over
any other forms of liberal education that may be available (and that
he criticizes as being negatively formulated or lacking in positive
content). Clearly, he is not concerned to provide just another of
many potential views on what constitutes liberal education. It
would seem then that Hirst is confronted by the epistemological
problem of explicating the true nature of knowledge by which educational practice ought necessarily to be advised.

However, the form of his theorizing makes epistemology an un-
comfortable and ultimately a dispensable (so it is claimed) endeavour. On the surface his position might appear as ambiguous in
the sense that it seems to trade on a seemingly incompatible combination of empiricism and a brand of Kantian idealism. He requires
that knowledge is available to us only through our conceptual schema
but also that his 'forms of knowledge' are in some sense a priori
conditions of those very schema. Concurrent with this framework
Hirst is at pains to reject both such epistemologies.

With reference to the nature of mind, he states that it is not
'some kind of organ or muscle'; it is not an 'entity' that can come
to conform with some external reality; 'it is rather that to have a
mind basically involves coming to have experience articulated by
means of various conceptual schema'. It might appear concretely
that in some senses we are in agreement; the achievement of education is to be seen that people can in their various ways produce a
shared world of performance. Education cannot be concerned with the
development of 'inner states' or the replication of mental
processes. This agreement is deceptive.

Hirst is also concerned to make explicit rejection of the 'a
priorist' view of knowledge - he alludes to this in that he con-
ceives of his 'forms of knowledge' as being socio-historical; that
is, they are the ways that we have over time come to understand.
(Perhaps here 'we' should be amplified into 'contemporary educated
Western man'.) (7) The forms of knowledge are to Hirst 'the basic
articulations whereby the whole of experience has become intelligi-

ble to man, they are the fundamental achievement of minds'. It is possible to detect a note of arrogance here in that the theorist is suggesting that his own analytic elections are in some vital way corresponding to the crucial achievement boundaries of our consciousness, i.e. mind within the philosopher's limits. Further, such a statement would seem to point to a version of knowledge as cumulative, as the past providing base lines for our forms of creativity and understanding. (8)

It is stressed that 'knowledge, however, must never be thought of merely as vast bodies of tested symbolic expressions'; however, while playing down an idealist conception Hirst is in fact still operating with his own form of a priori categories. His forms of knowledge, though historically and descriptively socially constructed, nevertheless take on an ahistorical and absolutist form in his contemporary theorizing. They are no longer seen to be on-going; they are in some way now seen to be constraining features of our world as knowledge. The community that generated the 'forms of knowledge' is the tradition of the past; the community that is the present is provided with a compelling legacy, so compelling that its own possibilities for discourse and the generation of knowledge remains unexplored or indeed curtailed. The 'forms' take on a kind of static facticity in that they are seen to be the determining features of the consciousness of individual members (determining, that is, if we allow the philosopher to reveal their logic to us). The freshly rendered, 'objective' nature of this conception of knowledge has provided for the 'forms' as being Durkheim-like 'social facts'; that is, they are characterized by 'externality', 'constraint' and 'normalcy'. (9) In this sense membership and community as concepts are denied, the social life as a generative 'theoretically' provided reality is denied and the very spirit of Wittgenstein's language games is denied.

To explain, understanding the use of words in language is analogous to understanding the rules of a game. If a player makes up new rules, or misapplies or misconceives the rules (in isolation), then the result is ambiguity and confusion just as in language. However, if the player treats the game as static and rule-governed, like the Durkheimian social bond, then he is also abusing the spirit of the game, namely in that it is an on-going activity, potentially bounded by rules-in-use. Further, the notion of rules-in-use can be conceptualized in terms of a member's expectations of the game within the game-in-progress. To be clear about language we must look to its uses, not to what it names. In this way Wittgenstein's own work is a series of investigations in progress; he is not working from basic propositions; he is not legislating for a static grasp; he is doing language-in-use.

It is not some exterior forms of knowledge that provide for 'forms of life'; on the contrary, the possibility of conceiving of forms of knowledge is only available through language games as displays of a 'form of life'. (10)

Hirst's denial of 'a priorist' views rests on his rejection of metaphysics. He states that it is publicly testable criteria of right and wrong that give objectivity to his 'forms of knowledge', and not some essential metaphysical realism. However, this does not constitute an absolute denial but only a shift of locus - it is

through the public criteria of testability imposed upon his present
non-generative community that he imports a new metaphysic. He is
saying that it is boundaries but not essences that define his
'forms'. The effect remains the same, the criteria are assumed as
absolutes, they are real, they are constraining. Perhaps the constraint appears softer, or just more hidden, but it is present - the
formulation remains positivistic, the 'criteria' may be equated with
nature's guiding hand. Further, the 'public' nature of the criteria
remains unexplored. Hirst refuses to confront the problem of the
indexical character of our language (presumably as criteria) in
social situations. We must assume that the idea of a 'public' is
imported to imply the social, and to give strength to his claims for
an unexplicated notion of 'consensus'.

A major problem for Hirst's formulations then, lies in his construction and necessary assumption of only one possible form of the
'forms of knowledge' - one set of forms leading to the 'self-
conscious rational mind of man'. In this sense he is non-reflexive
on his own practices of construction. His trouble would seem to
reside in his imposition and abuse of the notion of rationality,
which is necessarily a feature of the social grammar of performance
(in whatever possible society) and not a feature of a coherent non-
indexical logical life (whatever that might be?).

This leads us to call into question the implicit use of the
concept 'rationality' that underlies this problem. The notion of
'the rational mind of man' however it is articulated within the philosophy of education (as ultimately with reference to teaching-
learning as a practical accomplishment) is inevitably provided with
a wholeness, a constancy and a quality of possessing clearly identi-
fiable attributes - that is, it takes the form of a model. Such a
model of the rational life implicitly defines the way things are, or
could be, or even ought to be - or perhaps all of these things. It
could be said that all model-talk about education implies a sense of
how things (basically people) ought to be. As with much 'scientific
sociology', such models of 'rationality' as social action are conventionally characterized in terms of the inevitable logic of means-
ends schema - such that individual members as 'rational' fit within
a pre-established and more widely conceived social system of
'rationality': the world becomes intelligible to the theorist within
his coherent rational scheme, but the grounds of his scheme of
rationality remain unavailable to us.

From within such a position then, the theorist's scheme becomes a
resource and not a topic for analysis - the model, in this case
oriented by the 'forms of knowledge', is employed to reflect upon
the practices of members in their worlds; thus alternative versions
of liberal education (in this instance) are rendered as adequate/in-
adequate in relation to the extent to which they can be seen to
correspond with the philosopher's elections. In Garfinkel's (1967)
language, this method of addressing facets of a perceived reality as
'documents' of an underlying scheme (that of the theorist) produces
members as 'cultural dopes' in that they are perceived variously not
to comply with the inevitable logic of the model. As Hirst puts it
with reference to liberal education, 'It is a form of education
knowing no limits other than those necessarily imposed by the nature
of rational knowledge.' To demonstrate an ambiguity within Hirst's

position we may refer this back to his view of the 'forms' as being socio-historical constructs. He is caught by his own version of a cultural product - he is committed to 'rationality' as a cultural product yet he wishes to legislate for 'the rationality' as being external to and imposing upon the practices of men. (11)

Such a gloss on rationality is clearly highly ascriptive and normative. Hirst denies that it is a tautology to justify liberal education in terms of his 'rational forms of knowledge' - but we seem inevitably trapped within his model: if we are rational and our rationality is based on the 'forms' (as rational knowledge), then to ask for a justification of the 'forms' is presumably to act irrationally - or perhaps inconceivably!

My grasp of rationality as a sociologist requires that rationality be conceived of descriptively as a member's category, that is as displays of rationality or rationality-in-use. The problem of meaning dictates the label 'rational'; rationality can only apply or be applied to the meaning-giving activity of a member in a social context. So different meaning structures or rationalities exist according to different and various grammars of membership. We do not and we may not want to live within 'the rationality' that is Hirst's 'form of life'. Our language games are different (and various) - our rationality is only available in-use as intentional consciousnesses within the rules of our own particular language game.

As Schutz (1967) puts it, addressing rationality as an observer's category, 'rationality cannot be a peculiar feature of everyday thought, nor can it therefore be a methodological principle of interpreting human acts'. As such there can be no actions isolated as rational actions, there can only be systems of rational actions, that is language games or displays of membership. In Schutz's terms, Hirst's formulation can be no less of a 'cookbook recipe' than the infinite range of 'cookbook recipes' of 'rational action' that he is seeking to collect and remedy under his own.

This statement of difference does not lead me as theorist to make a special claim concerning my position on rationality; it is likewise no more than a gloss - however, my gloss is exposed as a topic for examination rather than concealed as a resource, unexplicated as such, which may be traded off for legislative purposes, such as those of Hirst. I seek not to impose alternative definitions of rationality upon members; rather I aim at making an authentic claim to the problematic status of my own procedure in constructing a version of rationality. Also, in Blum's (1970) terms, I aim at acknowledging that my descriptions of indexical performance are indexically tied to the conditions of their own occurrence. I am engaged in the social practice that is sociology, just as Hirst is engaged in the social practice of doing philosophy - our various performances demonstrate our different forms of membershipping. (12)

Hirst's model of rationality is a feature of the method that enables him to construct his 'logical relationship' - that between mind, knowledge and liberal education - and that which allows him to sidestep the metaphysical 'non-problems' of empiricist and idealist epistemologies. Thus: 'on logical grounds a consistent concept of liberal education must be worked out in terms of forms of knowledge. By this is meant, of course, not collections of information, but the complex ways of understanding experience that man has achieved, which are publicly specifiable and which are gained through learning'. However, as previously noted, the metaphysical problems that Hirst's form of analysis eschews it also necessarily assumes in the taken-for-granted definitions which provide the grounds for the newly articulated logical relationship.

Hirst's final statement revelation of the nature of his 'forms of knowledge', which are 'the basic articulations whereby the whole of experience has become intelligible to man, they are the fundamental achievement of mind', amounts to a list of seven finite categories. These categories, it is claimed, are all objectively testable, and further, each category possesses its own peculiar set of testing procedures (the criteria discussed earlier). They are then: (i) mathematics and formal logic, (ii) the physical (and natural) sciences, (iii) the human sciences and history, (iv) moral knowledge, (v) aesthetic knowledge, (vi) religious knowledge, and (vii) philosophy.

These 'forms' are specified as being all non-reduceable, although they are necessarily interrelated. Basic to, and behind, Hirst's notion of the development of mind is the development of an understanding of the relations between these categories with their own peculiar logically available objective testability (the 'realism' of the criteria). It must be noted that apparently the earliest formulation of these categories by Hirst saw history as apart from the human sciences (whatever they might constitute in order to recognize history as apart for naming or exclusion); and also that moral knowledge occupies the status of a 'field of knowledge' rather than that of a distinct 'form' or 'discipline'. (13) He adds the comment: 'it is the distinct disciplines that basically constitute the range of unique ways we have of understanding experience if to these is added the category of moral knowledge.' This is somewhat mystifying.

Note R.S.Peters's (1966) agreement in this context:
The structuring of knowledge into differentiated forms of thought and awareness is not an accidental or arbitrary matter, for there is no other way in which knowledge in depth can be developed. Mathematical concepts are different from moral, scientific, or religious ones; the criteria for truth and the methods of testing are different. There is however, a certain arbitrariness about what constitutes school subjects ... (14)
This constitutes a summary apologia for Hirst's main thesis.

In elucidating his forms of knowledge Hirst experiences some problems with the explication of their unique peculiar testing procedures - particularly with moral, aesthetic and religious knowledge. Hirst and Peters (1970) suggest that 'the precise nature of the grounds of our objective judgments in this area is not yet adequately understood'; perhaps 'more work needs to be done'. Presumably, until such time as religious or moral knowledge can be 'seen' (by whom?) to be as self-evidently and systematically autonomous as it is suggested by Hirst that formal logic is, then we must take it to be the case under the guidance of the philosophers' special knowledge - it is they who have conducted 'detailed studies' distinguishing the seven forms.

Commenting on Hirst's 'forms of knowledge', both Young (1971) and

Adelstein (1972) have noted that they 'appear' to be based upon some
kind of absolutist conception of a set of distinct categories, which
seem to correspond quite closely to the traditional areas of the
'academic' curriculum (leading to the 'educated man') and thus they
contribute to a justification rather than an examination of what are
no more than historically located social constructs. Here again
Hirst's ambiguity is demonstrated in these readings of his
statement, for they are offering criticism (ironically) in terms of
what he himself claims - namely that his 'forms' are socio-historical.

It must be restated that it is not 'subjects' that Hirst is addressing. Vis-a-vis the organization of knowledge, his forms are
'forms of understanding' which are apart from subject boundaries,
and they are by definition necessarily distinct. However, as Young
suggests, unless Hirst is willing to treat his necessary distinctions or intrinsic logics as problematic and provide explanations beyond a claim to the a priori, then his categories remain
arbitrary and commonsensical - and they certainly provide no more
than a relative statement with reference to curriculum planning.
(15)

In many ways Hirst's argument becomes more intelligible if read
as applying to subject boundaries; they are available as 'real'
organizational features; they present themselves as for-all-practi-
cal-purposes possibilities; and our recognition of them as bodies
of theories, information and types of procedure is more concretely
apparent and therefore less compulsive or deterministic than a
notion of external logically distinct 'forms' - however, this is not
Hirst's purpose.

If we take it that Hirst is operating with Wittgenstein's notion
of 'family resemblances' to assemble his 'forms', then certain
critical reflections need to be made. For Wittgenstein the expression 'family resemblances' was meant to convey the sense of
method involved in the theorist doing collection or categorization.
He says: 'And I shall say "games" form a family.' To treat things
as similar or as available for grouping is like commenting on family
resemblances. This is possible however only as or within a language
game; it is not a comment on the absolute nature of 'family resemblances'; it is a way of doing assembling 'in-language'. If I
assemble features of people, features of games or features of 'forms
of knowledge' and you do likewise we can talk about it; we may dis-
agree, we may even agree; however the assembling, collecting or
grouping, the 'forms' reside in our language (our form of life) of
the 'forms', not in some intrinsic essence outside of our discourse.
The possible similarities in our formulations are only as significant as the possible differences - boundaries are a feature of our
own method, our way of seeing (language).

Hirst, however, uses his method as assembling the forms but then
attempts to legislate for his method (as logical) as an absolutist
static grasp. His 'forms' become 'the forms', this is his statement
of positivism, his bid for a grasp of the 'objective'. The authenticity of his 'forms' would be assured if he acknowledged them as
being of his method, if he allowed for the possibility of difference - for as Wittgenstein puts it, 'the kinship is just as undenia-
ble as the difference'. From my reading however Hirst would be

using and abusing the expression 'family resemblances' as a feature of his method.

Through the idea of assembling I now consider Kuhn's (1970) notion of a 'paradigm', which, with reference to scientific knowledge (but by implication and for our purposes any 'forms' of knowledge), he takes to be an organized conceptual framework which provides for generating explanations as acceptable accounts within the scientific community. A paradigm is said to consist of standards, methods and a system of theory which derive their justi- fication from being grounded in certain metaphysical assumptions - that is, assumptions about the status of the phenomena being studied. This description of a paradigm provides an enlightening comment on Hirst's 'forms of knowledge' and 'categories of concepts'.

Walsh (1972), following Kuhn, suggests that a paradigm can be said to perform cognitive functions at three different levels: first, it suggests which entities nature does or does not possess; second, it provides a map of nature; and third, it provides pro- cedures by which the map of nature may be used to select what is relevant for further elaboration.

Kuhn's formulation is operating with a descriptive theory of the development of science. In the early stages of scientific investi- gation he suggests that there is a range or multiplicity of explana- tory theories, that there is no single theory - however, one such theory generally gains ascendancy through social acceptance in the scientific community. (Kuhn also notes that in pragmatic terms the social acceptability of a theory is not necessarily equated with its potential workability.) Thus a paradigm is generated and produces a tradition through the various forms of indoctrination of theory - i.e. available teachers, texts and materials, pressure on dis- senters, etc. A pre-paradigm stage is when no particular theory dominates a field; however, the stage of general acceptance of a single theory, 'the paradigm stage', is what he typifies as the period of 'normal science' (read 'normal knowledge'). Paradigm shifts, or the ascendancy of a new paradigm is a product of the 'crisis' generated within an existing paradigm, i.e. crisis as re- curring ambiguities, anomalies, confusion and anxiety. This now produces a stage typified as a scientific revolution, and the cycle begins again - crisis ⟶ pre-paradigm ⟶ new paradigm. Seen in terms of the history of science, Kuhn considers that the settled paradigm periods far outweigh the revolutionary periods; thus most science is seen as 'normal science' (science within a paradigm). For our purposes Hirst might be seen as not providing for the possi- bility of a crisis in his 'forms of knowledge'. He is operating at the first cognitive level of a paradigm; he is suggesting in the broadest terms what entities (as 'forms') nature does or does not possess; he is producing positivism as a paradigm and he is legis- lating for the permanent indubitable status of his 'forms' as the final, inevitable and indisputable paradigm. It is as if liberal education is to be constructed for all time in terms of giving the right kinds of answers to the right kinds of questions (that is, questions-answers within the 'forms'). It is as if the philosopher has placed limits upon the perception of mind and knowledge through the revelation of his objectivist 'forms'. Even disputing crisis,

it would seem that he does not provide for even micro-shifts (see
Kuhn's later micro-revolutions) that we might call shifts in
language game, because given Hirst's dominant (and imminent) 'forms'
'forms', discourse, as generative, is not possible.

It would seem then that Hirst's conception of liberal education
might become read as 'illiberal education', in the sense that, if
liberal education teaches what is (that is, knowledge bounded by the
rational 'forms'), then it is inescapable and circular; man is
without purpose or freedom - he becomes induced into the status quo.
(16) In a strong sense, all education conceived of as determined
beyond the social relations between members is illiberal, in that it
is only 'some men' that claim to have knowledge of the grounds of
the external determinant. Such a discussion would, however, take us
into talk about power and stratification - topics outside the scope
of ·this paper.

We may suppose that Hirst's kind of formulation, which apparently
makes steps towards outlining the structure of concepts and categories of knowledge, derives its appeal from its assumed capacity to
impose a 'constancy' or 'order' of a more than temporary nature on
the continuous character of experience. Such a position however
rests upon the non-reflexive acceptance of a model as 'real' and
'transcendent'. As a style of understanding it quite often provides
its own justification through an empiricist's mode of discourse,
that is through talk of proof, verification and testing (the
language of science), a discourse that can only be conducted in
terms of confirmation or rejection, a language restricted to 'yes'
and 'no'. As has been explicated in the field of sociology, (17)
such method and measurement (as testing) merely fashions the perceived world by its own procedures and systems of relevancies into
indices of its own preconstituted theoretical framework.

It is of course acknowledged that the practices of members in
social worlds produce working versions of 'order' and 'constancy' -
as social beings we are conscious of our experiences as within a
possible pattern. Concretely, the 'order' or structure of experiences that are a feature of our everyday lives is locatable only as
the potentially limitless social grammar of performance, i.e. as
expectations and rules-in-use by members in the business of being
members. However, order is not a concrete guiding character of the
world programmed by 'forms of knowledge': order is the analytic
character of the reflexive practices of members generating their
worlds through understanding.

It has been my intention to unravel Hirst's method of doing
'ordering'; that is, I have attempted to provide my way of constructing (as intelligible) Hirst's methods for producing his ideas
(forms of knowledge) as intelligible. As Blum (1970) puts it:
'What we want are the theorist's methods for the creation of his
idea, for it is in his production of the idea that his activity ac-
quires its analytic status as an instance of theorizing.'

This paper then has not, by design, amounted solely to a rebuttal
of Hirst's 'forms of knowledge' as being inadequate explanatory
constructs of our world. To do so my argument would have remained
within the concrete only; it would perhaps have offered alternative
epistemologies - this has not been the case. For our purposes the
'forms of knowledge' do not present themselves solely as constituted

in this manner; their character, for our form of theorizing, is
their character as the product of a chosen method of assembly. , In
attempting to explicate a sense of Hirst's methods I have addressed
his corpus of knowledge (i.e. one version of 'the corpus of educational knowledge as it has come to be formulated within the activity seen as the philosophy of education'); I have attempted to
explore the 'possible' nature of his theoretical elections. (18)

As was stated at the outset, one purpose of this paper was to
emphasize a sense of the theorist's own crucial involvement in the
production of knowledge (as displays of his mind and tradition). By
addressing these themes of 'mind' and 'knowledge' I have attempted
to demonstrate my involvement in doing the production of my 'mind'
and 'knowledge'. Further, I have throughout sought after a notion
of the production of a tradition in discourse with the reader.

To end, then, Hirst presents us with a closing-off, a position of
certainty from whence to stop doubting - in so doing he legislates
also for the concrete; he offers guidelines for practical action.
In return I offer an invitation to continue doubting and to pursue
the analytic in the face of the problematic - 'knowledge' and 'mind'
can then be seen in their proper place, as features of the analytic
doing (understanding) of human existence.

NOTES

1 See Heidegger (1970).
2 See Walsh's paper in this book with reference to science and sophisticated positivism as the 'correct form'.
3 Note R.S.Peters, 'Freedom and the development of the free man'
   in Doyle (1973, p.129): 'An example of such a limited form of
   development is given by Josephine Klein in her book "Samples
   from English Culture" (Routledge & Kegan Paul, 1965). She
   singles out certain abilities which are presupposed in the account of being a chooser given in section 1(ii) above. They are
   the ability to abstract and use generalizations, the ability to
   perceive the world as an ordered universe in which rational
   action is rewarded, the ability to plan ahead and exercise self-
   control. She cites evidence from Luria and Bernstein to show
   that the extent to which these abilities develop depends upon
   the prevalence of an elaborated form of language which is found
   in some strata of society, but not in others. She also shows
   how the beliefs and conduct of some working-class sub-cultures
   are affected by the arbitrariness of their child-rearing techniques. Such happy-go-lucky people have a stunted capacity for
   choice because the future has only limited relevance for them
   and because they are prejudiced, myopic, and unreflective in
   their beliefs.'
4 See here Gladwin (1971) and Keddie's paper in this book with
   reference to Gladwin.
5 See also Heidegger (1971) for statements concerning the nature
   of language, its richness and potential: 'Language as the House
   of Being.'
6 See Blum and McHugh (1971) for a similar analysis of the concept
   motive (within sociology).

7 See here Horton (1971) for articulations of non-Western (different) modes of providing intelligibility to experience.
8 Note Popper's position with reference to science; see also Walsh's paper in this volume.
9 We may note also that Durkheim's 'social facts' as rules of conduct are available to actors in their infringement or abuse. The 'factual' nature of the 'social' may be likened to prison walls that only present themselves as such if the inmate attempts to break through them. Think now of the 'forms of knowledge'.
10 This, I feel, resonates with Garfinkel's (1967) passage citing Wittgenstein: chapter 2, pp.70-1.
11 Drawing on the classical tradition, we might suggest that Weber (1964) was trapped by the same problem.
12 I recognize here that the sociology to which I make claim is the sociology of my own practice; it is my construction of a sociology that is demonstrated as this paper. I am aware that much sociology (and sociology-of-education) is done according to the (unreflexive) practices of Hirst's philosophizing.
13 To explain in Hirst's terms, 'fields' of knowledge refers to 'organizations of knowledge' which may be 'endlessly constructed according to particular theoretical or practical interests'. They are different in nature to the 'forms', which are particular, unique and distinct - and thus presumably not open to endless construction (necessarily).
14 See here Castaneda (1970) for a manifestly 'strange' 'structuring of knowledge into differentiated forms of thought and awareness', but one that is no more 'accidental or arbitrary'.
15 There is a further irony in this context if we note the comment of Hirst's editor Archambault: 'P.H.Hirst's paper, which closes the previous section, deals generally with the justification of subjects and the applications of them to educational practice.'
16 See Freire (1972).
17 See Cicourel (1964).
18 See Blum and McHugh (1971) for this sense of 'possible'.

ACKNOWLEDGMENTS

Thanks are offered to Dave Walsh for his reflections on the first draft of this paper, and to Mike Phillipson, Michael Young and Paul Filmer for their comments at a later stage.

BIBLIOGRAPHY

ADELSTEIN, D. (1972), The Philosophy of Education, or the Wisdom and Wit of R.S.Peters, in R.Paton (ed.), 'Counter Course', Penguin.
BLUM, A. (1970), Theorizing, in J.Douglas (ed.), 'Understanding Everyday Life', Routledge & Kegan Paul.
BLUM, A. and McHUGH, P. (1971), The Social Ascription of Motives, 'American Sociological Review', vol.36, no.1.
CASTANEDA, C. (1970), 'The Teachings of Don Juan - a Yaqui Way of Knowledge', Penguin.

CICOUREL, A. (1964), 'Method and Measurement in Sociology', New York, Free Press.
DOYLE, J.F. (1973), 'Educational Judgments', Routledge & Kegan Paul.
DURKHEIM, E. (1938), 'The Rules of Sociological Method', University of Chicago Press.
FREIRE, P. (1970), The Adult Literacy Process as Cultural Action for Freedom, 'Harvard Educational Review', vol.4, no.2.
FREIRE, P. (1972), 'Pedagogy of the Oppressed', Penguin.
GARFINKEL, H. (1967), 'Studies in Ethnomethodology', Englewood Cliffs, N.J., Prentice-Hall.
GLADWIN, T. (1971), 'East is a Big Bird', Cambridge, Mass., Harvard University Press.
HEIDEGGER, M. (1970), 'What is a Thing?', Chicago, Regnery Gateway.
HEIDEGGER, M. (1971), 'On the Way to Language', New York, Harper & Row.
HIRST, P.H. (1965), Liberal Education and the Forms of Knowledge, in R.D.Archambault (ed.), 'Philosophical Analysis and Education', Routledge & Kegan Paul.
HIRST, P.H. (1969), The Logic of the Curriculum, 'Journal of Curriculum Studies', vol.1, no.2.
HIRST, P.H. and PETERS, R.S. (1970), 'The Logic of Education', Routledge & Kegan Paul.
HORTON, R. (1971), African Traditional Thought and Western Science, in M.F.D.Young (ed.), 'Knowledge and Control', Collier-Macmillan.
KUHN, T. (1970), 'The Structure of Scientific Revolutions', University of Chicago Press.
McHUGH, P. (1970), On the Failure of Positivism, in J.Douglas (ed.), 'Understanding Everyday Life', Routledge & Kegan Paul.
PETERS, R.S. (1966), 'Ethics and Education', Allen & Unwin.
POPPER, K. (1963), 'Conjectures and Refutations', Routledge & Kegan Paul.
RYLE, G. (1949), 'The Concept of Mind', Hutchinson.
SCHUTZ, A. (1967), The Problem of Rationality in the Social World, in 'Collected Papers', vol.II, The Hague, Martinus Nijhoff.
WALSH, D. (1972), Varieties of Positivism, in P.Filmer et al., 'New Directions in Sociological Theory', Collier-Macmillan.
WEBER, M. (1964), 'The Theory of Social and Economic Organizations', New York, Free Press.
WITTGENSTEIN, L. (1953), 'Philosophical Investigations', Oxford, Blackwell.
WITTGENSTEIN, L. (1961), 'Tractatus Logico-Philosophicus', Routledge & Kegan Paul.
YOUNG, M.F.D. (1971), 'Knowledge and Control', Collier-Macmillan.

Chapter 4

SCIENCE, SOCIOLOGY AND EVERYDAY LIFE

David Walsh

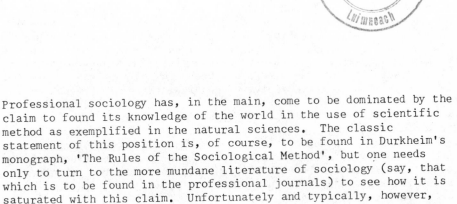

Professional sociology has, in the main, come to be dominated by the claim to found its knowledge of the world in the use of scientific method as exemplified in the natural sciences. The classic statement of this position is, of course, to be found in Durkheim's monograph, 'The Rules of the Sociological Method', but one needs only to turn to the more mundane literature of sociology (say, that which is to be found in the professional journals) to see how it is saturated with this claim. Unfortunately and typically, however, scientific method remains an unexamined resource for accounting the world in the hands of sociologists of a scientific persuasion. This I take to be a strange feature of their work in the sense that it remains the programmatic intent of sociology to hold the activities of members of the world to sociological account. By this I mean that sociology sees itself as engaged in the task of uncovering the ordered properties of those activities as socially occasioned productions. But presumably science, too, is just such an activity and subject to sociological report.

Why then do we find the absence of a sociological report on science by the practitioners of scientific sociology? I am not here trying to deny that scientific sociologists have written about science, (1) but that they do not treat the rationality of scientific method as a subject of sociological report, instead it is seen in a positivistic mode (2) i.e. as a set of context-free and hence objective procedures for capturing the underlying reality of the world. Such a position leads off from the question, 'How can we believe our eyes?' and finds its answer in a correspondence theory of truth. It relies on the assumption that there is a difference between the perceived objects of the outer world and the concrete objects themselves; i.e., the concreteness of objects is the property of those objects themselves and not of the ways in which they may be apprehended. The function of any conceptual scheme of categorization is, then, to render some sort of approximation to what is actually out there in the world. The possibility of rendering an approximation of what is out there in the world is seen to lie in the use of logico-empirical methods (i.e. scientific method) as unchanging universal and primary categories of apprehension which remain unaffected by the circumstances of the observer as far as the reproduction of the world is concerned. There is, therefore, in the correspondence theory of truth, a separation between the real world and the subjective interpretation of the world.

In this account of science, then, the scientist is seen to be, in Blum and McHugh's words, (3) a 'messenger of nature'. The task of the scientist is to provide a way in which nature can speak for itself. Ultimately, therefore, the validity of speech of the scientist is seen to reside in the claim that it is nature itself that authorizes his speech. Paradoxically, then, the scientist is forced to guarantee the validity of his speech by way of a denial of his authorship of it. (4) But since the decision as to whether it is nature that is speaking is grounded by the scientist in his methods (i.e. in his way of speaking) then, presumably, there is no other place than his methods to which we can look to locate the possibility and intelligibility of his (the scientist's) messages. It will be a feature of this paper to show, then, how science can be treated as a socially occasioned activity organized in terms of a set of practices for making the world visible, rational and reportable which grounds a community of observers (scientific members). In this sense scientific knowledge can be seen to be the managed accomplishment of the practitioners of science which is to say that the rationality of science is necessarily grounded in these socially occasioned methods. It will be argued further that the validity of scientific knowledge lies in the methods of science as publicly available grounds of sense.

I take it that this position expresses what I had earlier referred to as the programmatic intent of sociology, i.e. to hold the activities of members of the world to sociological account. The positivistic sociologist is caught on the horns of a dilemma of his own making. On the one hand, his commitment to sociology requires that he renders scientific procedures as subject to sociological description since they are members' activities (i.e., he has to show them to be socially occasioned procedures). Yet on the other hand, his commitment to positivism forces him to treat these procedures as context-free; i.e., they are unchanging universal and primary categories of apprehension which are unaffected by the (socially occasioned) circumstances of the observer. For the positivist to take up the programmatic intent of sociology on this occasion would require him to show the socially contextual character of scientific rationality and consequently would call into question his own production on precisely these grounds. The positivist can sustain the validity of his enterprise as a constructive sociology (5) only so long as he treats science and the scientific method as an unexamined resource on which he can draw for the production of his own accounts. This, then, is the reason why we find the absence of a sociological report on scientific methods by the practitioners of scientific sociology.

Let us go back and attempt to constitute our account of science in consideration of a quite different question from that of the positivist, viz. in the question, 'How do we believe our eyes?' We will make it a feature of our sociological description of science, then, that it reports unscientific method as scientific members' procedures for deciding this question. It will be our concern to show how how the scientist attends to the objects of his inquiry in terms of some set of socially sanctioned rules of inference. In this respect we can draw upon the important insights that Kuhn's (1970a) work has made available on how science gets done without subscribing to the qualitative distinction that he draws between science and everyday common sense.

Kuhn has suggested that science is describable in terms of the interpretive practices by which its members make sense of the natural world. These practices he labels as scientific paradigms: 'a scientific paradigm stands for the entire constellation of beliefs, values, techniques and so on shared by the members of a given community' (Kuhn, 1970a, p.175). A feature, then, of any paradigm is that it not only prescribes some set of methodological rules which define the appropriate (and thereby legitimate) ways in which the scientist is to conduct his investigations but that it also prescribes the character of the universe which is the subject of investigation and with reference to which these rules find their legitimate application. In this sense, then, the criteria of truth and validity are part and parcel of the paradigm itself. Any paradigm carries as embedded features within itself, therefore, the answers to such critical questions as: 'What are the fundamental entities of which the universe is composed? How do these interact with each other and in what sense? What questions may be legitimately asked about such entities and what techniques employed in seeking solutions?' (Kuhn, 1970a, pp.4-5) A paradigm constitutes, then, a common scheme of reference or set of background expectancies that provides the taken-for-granted world of the scientist who operates from within it. The generation of scientific knowledge is, therefore, a paradigmatic induced affair in the sense that scientific practitioners manage its production according to the routine grounds of inference and interpretation that are commonly available within the paradigm.

A scientific paradigm locates some set of rules (i.e. a language) for transforming commonsense phenomena into the thought-objects or facts of science, and in that sense they are constitutive of those objects. Strictly speaking, there are no such things as facts pure and simple. All facts are from the outset selected from a universal context by the activities of our mind. They are always interpreted facts which rely for their intelligibility on the interpretational context through which they are generated as facts at all. In, say, the case of quantum physics even the material dimensions of the phenomena into which it inquires are brought into question as a feature of the mathematical character of the formulation in terms of which it proceeds. It becomes a characteristic of this linguistic usage that it abandons altogether the notion that the phenomena to which it is addressed (e.g. nucleons, protons, electrons) are material facts in favour of a formulation of them as possibilities expressed in terms of mathematical symbols. The world of quantum physics is a world that lacks the dimensions of space and time and the phenomena under investigation are not describable in terms of any of the concepts of classical physics such as size, energy, location and velocity. To appropriate the world through a scientific language is, then, to provide for a specific formulation of the real character of that world in which the intelligibility of that formulation is located exclusively in the rules by which it is produced. Such an appropriation, as an activity of mind, is what I take to be the activity of theorizing. That is, we can describe theorizing as an activity that proceeds in accord with an organized set of procedures for the production of knowledge whereby phenomena are transformed within a normative order that sets them in a context and makes sense of them. A scientific language is just such a set of procedures which supplies the rules of transformation that provide for their own sense of adequacy by way of a description of events that produces them as events in accord with the rules of transformation. To put this another way, it is to show that it is the activity of theorizing that provides for the real (the factual, the concrete) and not the reverse. Now, whereas this may not be an inordinate point to understand as far as science is concerned, it happens also to be a feature of everyday reasoning too. I assume this to be part of the intended sense of Garfinkel's remark that 'the activities whereby members produce and manage settings of organized everyday affairs are identical with members' procedures for making those settings account-able' (Garfinkel, 1967, p.1). But everyday understanding is something I wish to turn to at a later point. (6)

Now to call attention to the linguistic appropriation of the world by science is to call attention to the socially organized character of that appropriation. More particularly, it is to call attention to two necessary features of this or any other socially organized linguistic appropriation or account of the world, viz. how that appropriation is both context-bound (i.e. 'indexical' in character) and 'reflexively' organized (i.e. derives its intelligibility from the interpretive procedures that do the work of appropriation). Such procedures are unavoidably and inextricably located in (indeed, they are actually constitutive of) the language that any account consists of and without which the language would not be sensible (meaningful) and thus not even a language at all. How then might we address the claim of the natural sciences to be an objective discourse if objective in this instance makes reference to the substitution of universal statements for indexical expressions? Here I would suggest that the process of substitution has to be seen as the application of a public (i.e. consensually) constitutive method to the world which provides for a common reading of that world by all members who use the method. Thus it is not that scientific formulations of the world are context-free that makes them 'objective', but rather the fact that they are grounded in the context of a conventionally understood and institutionalized body of public practices, i.e. the scientific paradigm. Such practices themselves constitute formulations (which are thus rationally observable as scientific formulations) which provide for a way of talking about the world that can be treated as an objective way of talking about it in so far as that way of talking about it constitutes it as a natural world, i.e. in so far as that constitution lends to objects of the natural world their 'naturalness'.

The possibility of natural sciences as a stipulative enterprise is located in the inherent meaninglessness of the natural world. There is no manner in which the scientist could address the objects of that world other than by a constitutive exercise generated from out of his cognitive concerns. The requirements of science, then, come to turn not on the natural world as such but rather on the creation of a public language of discourse through which science can proceed as organized and controlled inquiry and which allows the scientist to talk of it 'as such' (everyday talk does the same work too). These requirements find their satisfaction in the generation of a language by scientists that subscribes (at least at the level of the publication of materials) (7) to the canons of logico-empirical inquiry. We are talking here then of the intended sense of the scientists' own words when they refer to 'good scientific practice', i.e. to the way in which they make science rationally observable as such. It becomes a feature, therefore, of scientific constructs which are candidates for entry into the rationally observable discourse of scientists (i.e. which are candidates for recognition as science at all) that they be framed in such a manner as to make them both internally consistent and anchored in rules for the observation of data by way of which such data can be referred back and made demonstrably recognizable. Such is the process of verification in the natural sciences. Moreover, such constructs should be, wherever possible, framed in a manner suitable for the purposes of measurement. A characteristic feature of the natural sciences has been the success with which they have developed measurement techniques yielding numerical data as the operational counterparts of the constructs of scientific modes. They introduce a high degree of clarity into the theoretical propositions or into the comprehensive theoretical systems and allow for a greater degree of precision in the procedures of testing such theories. But (and this returns us to the problem of reflexivity which has already been mentioned) we need to remember that measurement presupposes a bounded network of shared meanings and it is precisely these shared meanings that a scientific paradigm provides. (8)

Validation is grounded in the natural sciences in terms of agreed procedures of verification centring around the operations of systematic observation, replication and prediction. The data are treated as a preconstituted object world, the overt and manifest characteristics of which are determined by a particular formulation of it. Thus the concepts and theories of science operate as a system of hypotheses that are tested by deducing the logical consequences from a set of general postulates and some set of specific assumptions and comparing these with records of observations regarded as empirical counterparts of the specific assumptions and the specific consequences. Let us take the example of Dalton's Atomic Theory and the Law of the Conservation of Mass to make this point clearer. Dalton's Atomic Theory formulates an atomic model of the material world in which the constitutive features of that world are axiomatically defined as part of the formulation. So, according to this model, matter consists of atoms; atoms are indestructible and indivisible; and each element has atoms of different weights. The concept of weight is drawn from Newtonian physics. Following these axiomatic assumptions we can deduce the following consequence, which is that in any chemical reaction matter cannot be created or destroyed (the Law of the Conservation of Mass). The Law can be made subject to empirical demonstration by way of an experiment that involves inducing a chemical reaction in some element and using Newtonian principles to construct a balancing apparatus to record and measure the weight of that element before and after the chemical reaction is induced. Here weight has to be taken, for all practical purposes, as an index of mass since mass itself cannot be made subject to measurement. So, for example, if one burns magnesium metal with oxygen to produce magnesium oxide, the weight of the magnesium oxide that is produced should be the same as that of the magnesium and the oxygen before burning. A demonstration that this is the case would stand, therefore, as a good enough empirical confirmation of the Law and the theory from which it is derived. Such a demonstration can, of course, be subjected to continual repetition. Moreover, the experimental nature of that demonstration provides for the conditions of its control.

However, the example points to something altogether more significant, viz. how the empirical particulars that are observed in the experimental situation cannot be divorced from the theoretically informed procedures by which they are decided. In other words, this example of verification in science indexes a concrete demonstration of the insoluble problematics of linguistic reflexivity in the sense that the verification procedures that are adduced to test an hypothesis are assembled and formulated in precisely the same terms as the hypothesis that they are designed to test. As such it raises the altogether interesting question of how the verification procedures of science may be said to constitute a test of the validity of scientific explanations. Popper has argued a solution to this problem in terms of the principle of falsification. He suggests that, since successfully predicted outcomes can never logically guarantee the validity of the theory from which they are derived, then methodic concern must be turned instead to a reversal of this logic, viz. that a denial of a consequence of a theory ipso facto denies the theory of which it is derived. A theory, then, that is incapable of falsification should not be admitted into science at all. The problem with the principle of falsification is, however, one which Kuhn points to. It requires that 'we produce the class of all logical consequences of the theory and then choose from among these, with the aid of background knowledge, the classes of all true and all false consequences ... None of these tasks can, however, be accomplished unless the theory is fully articulated logically and unless the terms through which it attaches to nature are sufficiently defined so as to determine their applicability in all possible cases' (Kuhn, 1970b, p.16). No scientific theory attempts to undertake such an impossible task of total explication: rather the scientific paradigm is used to bridge the gap between the content of a theory and its application. Moreover, this is a point with which Popper himself concurs since he remarks in 'The Logic of Scientific Discovery' (1959) that no conclusive disproof of a theory can ever be adduced since 'it is always possible to say that experimental results are not reliable and that the discrepancies which are asserted to exist between the experimental results and the theory are only apparent and that they will disappear with the advance of our understanding' (p.50). In the case of the experimental demonstration of the Law of the Conservation of Mass, where weight is seen to differ as a result of inducing a chemical reaction, this difference would be probably treated by chemists as due to a faulty balance.

This returns us, then, to the central argument concerning the constitutive character of scientific practice. Everyday scientific

activity prefers to use the practice of systematic observation for
purposes of confirmation. It is concerned with appraising empirical
particulars within a chosen and continuously elaborated conceptual
framework (Kuhn refers to this everyday scientific activity as
puzzle-solving). In these terms the scientist is able to locate invariant properties within the world of nature and hence to ground
his enterprise as the explication of that invariance. But, as Harre
(1964) makes clear,

> invariances are not at all obvious in nature and cannot be demon-
> strated in any obvious way by experiment. It is not clear how
> one would demonstrate experimentally that momentum is conserved
> in a certain sort of interaction. This cannot be done by sepa-
> rating off momentum and measuring it independently of the bodies
> which 'possess' it, for momentum is the product of mass and ve-
> locity and these are quite different sorts of bodily properties.
> Clearly the origin of the invariances is not to be found in the
> experimental side of science. It is to be found in the general
> conceptual system. (p.32)

So the methodological requirement that scientific theories be empirically verifiable in the sense that they should constitute
general statements concerning the relationship between events that
assert either the conditions sufficient or necessary or both for the
occurrence of certain types of events implies an understanding that
what is necessary and what is sufficient is determined by the system
of relevancies of the scientific paradigm itself.

The notion of invariance as a reflexively organized feature of
the methodological procedures of the scientist allows us, in turn,
to locate the methodic character of prediction in the natural
sciences as a kind of self-fulfilling prophecy. To quote Harré
again:

> prediction depends upon having a rule which usually works, and to
> have a rule a necessary condition is that it be applied suc-
> cessfully more than once. But for there to be a second appli-
> cation of a rule there must be some invariance either in process,
> substance, or property which persists from the first application
> of the rule to the second and subsequent applications, as the in-
> variance of momentum is a characteristic of mechanical changes.
> (p.33)

Now, in so far as invariance is the outcome of the way in which the
scientist conceptualizes the world into which he inquires, then prediction is unavoidably a kind of self-fulfilling prophecy. If this
were not so, then the paradigm that the scientist employs would presumably not appear to provide for the constitution or explanation of
anything and would, in that sense, not be recognizable as a paradigm
at all. An interesting consequence that follows from this is that
the failure to effectuate the predicted results on the part of some
scientist who is using a particular paradigm is often laid at his
door by fellow scientists rather than at the door of the paradigm he
is using. At the most that failure may be treated as an occasion to
articulate the paradigm a little further. This has to be so because
the other alternative would be to reject the paradigm altogether as
an effective source for generating explanations of those phenomena
which have been constituted by it as explicable phenomena in the
first place. But this would be an unpalatable alternative for most

journeymen scientists since it is the paradigm under whose aegis
they practise that grounds the legitimacy of a community of professional scientists as recognizably professional scientists engaged
in recognizably scientific work. Thus we are returned to the ways
in which public consent grounds scientific inquiry as a rational
enterprise, i.e. how the validity of scientific knowledge lies in
the methods of science as publicly available grounds of sense.

Popper finds, in the public character of science, a methodic solution to the question of how the socially organized practice of
changing a scientific paradigm gets done in terms of the free and
open testing of scientific theories. Paradigmatic change becomes
for him, then, rationally observable and accountable as 'the sur-
vival of the fittest' by way of which a corpus of scientific
knowledge gets cumulatively assembled. However, his methodic solution chooses to ignore the normative context of science. A scientific paradigm performs not only cognitive functions but also normative functions, i.e. it not only provides a map of nature but also
gives directions for map-making. Now, if we see that scientific advance constitutes a radical revision of the corpus of knowledge
(say, for example, a move from Ptolemaic to Copernican astronomy),
then that advance is rationally observable as the replacement of one
set of directions for map-making by another, i.e. a change from one
paradigm to another. But the Popperian claim to find the rule for
scientific advance in the everyday scientific activities of replication and testing fails to account for that replacement. As the
replacement of one paradigm by another involves a significant shift
in the criteria determining the legitimacy of both problems and proposed solutions, the process of choosing between paradigms cannot be
settled in terms of the criteria of everyday scientific activity
(vide Popper) since these kinds of criteria remain securely tied to
the particular paradigms from which they are derived. Rather the
choice has to be made upon answers to the question of which problem
it is more significant to have solved and such answers are based
upon values external to normal everyday science. It is this then,
the normative character of scientific paradigms, which Kuhn seizes
upon to render scientific advance as observable and accountable in
terms of revolution.

Moreover, it is to the normative character of scientific paradigms that we must turn if we are to place the role of discovery in
scientific advance. It is only because the paradigm, as a way of
seeing the world, prepares the scientist not to see features of that
world that discovery is intelligible and observable at all. A discovery then, is a violation of paradigmatic-induced expectations;
it is an anomaly within a paradigm. As such, it provides the occasion for a further articulation of the paradigm that grounds the
normal routine scientific activity of puzzle-solving (I use Kuhn's
term) by the practitioners of that paradigm. Only by bringing dis-
coveries within the bounds of some scientific paradigm do they take
on the character of intelligible scientific facts at all. However,
although puzzle-solving may provide the routine stuff of everyday
scientific activity, the piling up of anomalies may at a certain
point bring about a crisis situation in a paradigm where the practitioners of that paradigm begin to lose faith in its explanatory
potency and begin the search for another. So, for example, Ptole-

maic astronomy had long been in a situation of crisis before Copernicus as it struggled to articulate its paradigm in respect of
observations with regard to both planetary position and the pro-
cession of the equinoxes to the point at which it was hopelessly
complex but still inaccurate in its predictions and ridden with discrepancies. Or again, phlogiston theory was precipitated into a
state of crisis during the eighteenth century in its attempt to explain why some bodies increased in weight when they were burned or
roasted. (9) In both cases, the crisis was resolved only when a new
paradigm had been formulated to replace the old, in the first case
the Copernican heliocentric system of astronomy and in the second
the oxygen theory of combustion.

Now it is important to see a number of features in the replacement of one paradigm by another. First, the emergence of a-
nomalies, even in large numbers, within a paradigm in the form of
counter-instances is not in itself sufficient to lead practitioners
of that paradigm to abandon it. A paradigm is not rejected unless a
new paradigm has been constituted which will substitute for it.
This has to be so because the rejection of a paradigm without the
substitution of an alternative on the part of practitioners would be
the same as to abandon doing science altogether since (as has been
pointed out earlier) it is the commitment to practice in terms of
some paradigm that makes that practice recognizably observable as
scientific practice at all. Moreover, anomalies or counter-
instances only take on the character of scientific facts by virtue
of their subsumption with a paradigm. The emergence of anomalies as
such within a paradigm where no alternative is on the horizon merely
leads practitioners of that paradigm to articulate it a little
further so as to bring those anomalies within its scope. So, for
example, the discovery of oxygen by Priestley did not lead him to
abandon the phlogiston theory but rather to articulate that theory
further to cover his discovery which he incorporated into that
theory as dephlogisticated air. It was not until Lavoisier proposed
an entirely new theory that oxygen could be incorporated into
science as precisely just that, viz. oxygen; in other words, the
recognizability of oxygen awaited a reassembly of the corpus of
knowledge itself.

This, then, brings us to the second feature of the replacement of
one paradigm by another, viz. that this process of replacement is
recognizably observable as a process of re-theorizing the world. In
other words, the scientist who formulates a new paradigm comes to
see the world quite differently from the way he saw it before which
means that what he sees within it is altogether different too. The
switch from Priestley's dephlogisticated air to Lavoisier's oxygen
was not, therefore, some kind of cumulative addition to an on-going
body of knowledge but the outcome of a completely new vision of the
world. It required the effort of re-theorizing the world to incorporate oxygen as a recognizable feature of it. I take this to be
the sense of Kuhn's point when he refers to Priestley and Lavoisier:
'the fact that a major paradigm revision was needed to see what
Lavoisier saw must be the principal reason why Priestley was, to the
end of his long life, unable to see it' (Kuhn, 1970a, p.56). Now
whereas the recognition of a growing situation of crisis by the
practitioners of a paradigm (say, in the form of mounting anomalies

and ineffective attempts to shore the paradigm up) may act as the background circumstances in terms of which a new paradigm is forged, there are no rules within the routines of puzzle-solving that provide a methodic formula for doing the work of forging it. In this sense, the activity of re-theorizing takes an ad hoc quality whereby the scientist is willing to seize upon whatever will give him a purchase upon the problem that he seeks to resolve. In seeking to rediscover nature, then, the scientist now has to undertake to recover the grounds of theorizing as an intelligible activity by addressing once again his own tradition of rationality which is science, and wherein nature is apprehended. That is to say, the scientist if forced to take up the question of the reflexivity of his own accounts.

The ad hoc quality of particular efforts of re-theorizing comes to the fore, for example, in the emergence of the Copernican system of astronomy where the rediscovery and the rise of Neoplatonism played a major part in providing Copernicus with a way of addressing the acknowledged failures of the Ptolemaic system such as to allow to engage in a reconceptualization of the universe at this point. Or again, Watson (1968) recounts how he and Crick produced the discovery of DNA and created a new paradigm as the outcome of the interplay between atomic model construction, abstract mathematical speculation and laboratory findings in which the first two predominated since they provided them with a way of coming to see the character of the latter. (10)

Moreover, both examples point to something else of particular importance, viz. that, although the scientist has to display nature in that which wants to show, elegance and economy can count as very good grounds for accepting a paradigm. So, for example, Kuhn writes: 'in the 16th century Copernicus' co-worker, Domenico da Novara, held that no system so cumbersome and inaccurate as the Ptolemaic had become could possibly be true of nature. And Copernicus himself wrote in the preface to the 'De Revolutionibus' that the astronomical tradition he had inherited had finally created only a monster' (Kuhn, 1970a, p.69). What the Copernican system provided was elegance and economy but not necessarily a greater degree of accuracy in every area of application by comparison with the Ptolemaic system. Or again, Watson writes of a fellow scientist viewing the model of DNA that: 'nonetheless, like almost everyone else, she saw the appeal of the base pairs and accepted the fact that the structure was too pretty not to be true' (Watson, 1968, p.210).

We are returned, then, through this discussion of scientific advance in terms of re-theorizing the world (the replacement of one paradigm by another), to the ways in which science is grounded as a recognizable and observable activity by the use of a paradigm on the part of scientific practitioners. Everyday normal scientific activity is activity conducted within a socially negotiated interpretive framework i.e. by way of a body of procedures recognized as 'scientific' by the practitioners themselves. A scientific explanation is, then, objective only in the sense that it grasps those aspects of the world that are relevant from the point of view of that body of procedures since they are constitutive of scientific method. To quote McHugh (1970, p.332):

Nothing - no object, event or circumstance - determines its own

> status as truth, either to the scientist or science. No sign
> automatically attaches a referent, no fact speaks for itself, no
> proposition for its value. A nude proposition is without any
> immanent status, because its truth value cannot be assessed by
> observing its relation to a datum ... Rather, just as an event
> comes to be intelligible to the scientist only after applying to
> it some rule of grammar - a proposition comes to be knowledge
> only after conceiving it in terms of some rule of the canon that
> depicts the linguistic procedure by which the proposition is
> given life as a course of institutional action.

Thus the universalistic claim of scientific formulations glosses the
necessary reliance of these formulations upon a tacit understanding
of the relevancies in terms of which they are constructed and in
terms of which they receive their intelligibility. However, this is
not a problem for the natural sciences in so far as they frankly
recognize the stipulative character of their enterprise - their concern is not with some kind of ultimate truth about the natural world
but with the adequacy of formulations of that world to their own
purposes. The natural sciences need only to guarantee the rationality of their own discourse as a publicly available method of
making sense in order for them to proceed successfully.

What now becomes problematic is whether the constitutive
programme of the natural sciences can be seen to describe a suitable
set of procedures for the appropriation of the social world.
'Scientific' sociologists seem to have no doubts on the matter:
witness the manner in which Durkheim's injunction to treat social
facts as things is commonly followed. (11) What gets passed over
in such an injunction is that the social world has already been appropriated, i.e. the very availability of the social world lies in
its constitution by the glossing practices of its members. It has
been pre-selected and pre-interpreted by its members in terms of the
everyday talk and treatment by which they apprehend, display and
regularly confirm the events, actions and appearances within it. In
this respect we can return to what I have treated as describable
features of scientific accounts and show them to be observable
features of all accounts of the world whether lay or scientific. It
is a feature of my display of scientific accounts to show how they
are practically accomplished by the use of a socially situated
method (i.e. a special language) for describing the natural world
whereby the events of that world are transformed in accord with the
rules of that method and made reportable and observable as such.
Socially situated here refers to the ways in which the recognizable
sense of any scientific account is indexically and reflexively tied
to the occasions on which that special language is used to describe
events within the world. Now it is part of my argument to show that
lay members use natural language to accomplish the work of making
sense of the world in which that accomplishment is, like the above,
indexically and reflexively tied to the occasions on which it is
used. In other words, through the routine application of everyday
talk and treatment to the world, lay members provide for the de-
monstrable intelligibility of that world, i.e. they make social life
a coherent, rational and comprehensible reality for themselves.
Just as a scientific language assembles a corpus of scientific
knowledge which provides the routine grounds for making scientific
sense of the world, so natural language assembles a corpus of

everyday commonsense knowledge which provides the routine grounds of
inference and interpretation commonly available to lay members for
making sense of the world.

To detail this a little more, the corpus of scientific knowledge
(a scientific paradigm) locates both a context and a language for
framing scientific accounts, and these accounts trade upon that
language (reflexivity) and that context (indexicality) to make
sense. In this way, we can treat what is taken to be the hallmark
of science, viz. the substitution of objective for indexical expressions, by making that substitution visible and reportable as the
practical accomplishment of scientists using a publicly available
method for reading the natural world and bringing it off as such.
Now commonsense reasoning has precisely this character too. The
corpus of commonsense knowledge locates both a context and a
language (natural language) by way of which lay members can come to
frame everyday accounts of the world. In using that corpus as an
everyday public method for making sense of the world, then, lay
members achieve a similar substitution of objective for indexical
expressions as a feature of the way in which they assemble it. So
the claim that sociology has special knowledge of the social world
by virtue of the ways in which it substitutes objective sociological
expressions for lay indexical expressions through the use of the
scientific method comes to ignore a number of things. First, it
ignores the way in which scientific method is itself a practical
accomplishment, i.e. a socially situated production. Second, it
ignores the ways in which that substitution is already accomplished
by lay members in terms of the reflexively organized everyday accounts of the world which necessarily typify the features of that
world for them; and third, it ignores the ways in which the 'objective' accounts of 'scientific sociology are themselves a practical accomplishment. So the 'scientific' sociologist fails to see
how his own describing practices are constitutive of the world they
address in the sense that they provide for the intelligibility of
those empirical particulars that he apprehends as features of the
real world. Moreover, in choosing to deny the reflexively organized
features of his own accounts in favour of a naive reliance on the
undoubted factual character of the world that they reveal, the sociologist comes to share exactly the same stance towards the world as
that of lay members themselves. That is, the scientific sociologist
now finds himself engaged in a competition with lay members to
reveal the true underlying character of the social world in which
the real features of that world are taken to lie somewhere outside
of the methods by which they came to be appropriated in the first
place.

In this sense lay and sociological accounts of the social world
become indistinguishable from one another. The substitution of
formal sociological expressions for lay indexical expressions in
documenting the social world does not alter the fact that the intelligibility of the appearances that come to be so documented is
the practical accomplishment of the interpretive procedures that do
this work of substitution. In other words, the recognizable sense
of any sociological account is the product of the reflexive organization of that account itself. 'Scientific' sociologists choose to
ignore the reflexivity of their own accounts by assuming that the

translation of these accounts into a scientific language somehow
guarantees their objective neutrality and allows them to tap the
reality that underlies the appearances of the world.

What is interesting is how that substitution that claims to
effect a distinction between lay and sociological reasoning is
everywhere grounded in the sociologist's own common membership of
society, which supplies him not only with the topic of enquiry but
also with a resource by which to explicate it. That is to say, the
claim on the part of the sociologist to have suspended his membership of society in order to be scientific about it actually glosses
the ways in which his interpretive procedures are grounded in the
use of natural language and consequently remain indexically and reflexively tied to everyday membership and the corpus of commonsense
knowledge. So, for example, an election to treat the causes of
crime or suicide or poverty already preserves a commonsense understanding of these phenomena as features of the real world. The use
of official statistics by the sociologist to make the factual basis
of these phenomena more apparent merely reinforces that commonsense
understanding. In other words, to assume the availability of those
phenomena as topics of sociological enquiry is to use 'what anybody
knows about society' who is a member of it as a way of making those
phenomena visible and reportable as such. In doing so it fails to
display the ways in which commonsense reasoning uncovers these
phenomena and renders them visible and reportable.

Commonsense reasoning, then, forms the background knowledge in
terms of which the sociologist researches the world and makes sense
of it. His use of a specialized vocabulary is merely a translation
of everyday usages which does not transform them into an objective
discourse but merely into a gloss on 'what anybody knows'. Moreover, it is precisely because sociological accounts are grounded in
everyday usages that they become reports upon the social world at
all since that world is, itself, constituted and made available by
such usages. Now the important consequence of this last remark is
that it raises all members of the world to the status of sociological observers of it in which no one group can claim to have privi-
leged access to an understanding of it. So the generation of lay
members of the world as 'cultural dopes' who fail to grasp the reality of the social world which the rational model of sociology lays
bare only serves to disguise the ways in which that model is itself
the outcome of practical reasoning on the part of the sociologists.
How the sociologist brings off his sense of the real world in terms
of his method is clearly observable in, for example, the use of
questionnaire schedules in which questions are designed to elicit
responses that will, in turn, uncover the reality underlying the appearances of the world. However, the very activity of designing a
schedule incorporates the sociologist's own sense of social
structure which then comes to provide a procrustean bed into which
responses can be forced by the sociologist on the assumption that
respondents share his sense of social structure. In other words,
the claim that his schedule taps the underlying reality of the world
assumes a whole set of correspondences. First, it assumes a correspondence between the indicators used by the respondent to identify
meaningful objects and events and the indicators used by the sociologist to identify meaningful objects and events. Second, it as-

sumes a correspondence between the respondent's point of view and
the sociologist's point of view; i.e. they are assumed to share the
same language and meanings to subsume observations and experiences.
And third, it assumes a correspondence between the normative rules
governing the respondent's perception of his environment and the
theoretical and methodological rules governing the sociologist's
perception and interpretation of the same environment.

In these ways, then, the practices of 'scientific' sociology
begin to lose their point since the claims that are made for them in
terms of some professional 'pay-off' remain unfounded since the
substitution of formal sociological expressions for lay indexical
expressions is everywhere a practical accomplishment. The competition between sociology and everyday common sense to determine the
objective reality of the social world becomes, therefore, an absurd
contest. Instead, this paper has proposed and attempted to imple-
ment an examination of science that preserves the programmatic
intent of sociology, which is to hold all the activities of members
of the world to sociological account. In this sense I have made it
my task to show how scientific enquiry shares the mundane features
of all enquiry by virtue of the ways in which it is grounded in
common membership. All enquiry, whether lay, scientific or sociological, is the socially situated practices of members of the world
for making sense of that world and is, by virtue of this, observable
and recognizable as practical reasoning. Now this claim to show the
mundane features of all enquiry is not a claim that exempts my own
from displaying the same. It is not a feature of that display that
it incorporates a suspension of membership, since there is no way in
which enquiry could be sustained except through membership, i.e. the
very possibility and intelligibility of enquiry is grounded by
membership. Rather it is a claim that asserts my membership within
the theoretic community of sociology. To give expression to the
programmatic intent of sociology is, then, to address the tradition
of rationality which is indexed by that intent by way of a description of events that assembles them according to the rule of
reflexivity which the tradition recommends. The central feature of
this task has been, therefore, an implementation of the ethnomethod-
ological recommendation of Garfinkel (1967) that 'the activities
whereby members produce and manage settings of organised everyday
affairs are identical with members' procedures for making those
settings accountable' (p.1) by showing the indexical and reflexive
properties of those procedures in scientific, lay and sociological
enquiry.

ACKNOWLEDGMENTS

I am particularly indebted to my colleague at Goldsmiths' College,
Paul Filmer, for his extremely invaluable comments on an earlier
draft of this paper. I have tried to incorporate many of them into
its final form. Chris Jenks and Michael Phillipson of Goldsmiths'
College and Michael Young of the Institute of Education of the University of London have also made major contributions to my attempt
to clarify many of the issues discussed in the paper through the
various discussions I have had with them. They are not to be

blamed, however, for the content of the paper that was finally
drafted by myself.

NOTES

1 See Barber (1952).
2 I refer here to the position of logical positivism.
3 Part of the argument that follows relies on my reading of some
   of the ideas generated in the seminars held at Goldsmiths'
   College in 1971-2 by Peter McHugh and Alan Blum.
4 It is interesting to note in passing that the denial of speech
   as his speech by the positivistic scientist would make of him
   the paradigm case of 'alienated man', according to the Marxist
   version of alienation.
5 Constructive sociology is here referred to as that kind of sociology which, in slang parlance, claims to 'tell it like it is'
   by revealing the reality that underlies appearances, whereas it
   would be my claim that this revelation is a positive production
   of sociologists' own methodic procedures. In other words, the
   world they reveal is only their world.
6 One might note the difference here between my formulation of the
   genesis of knowledge and the Marxist thesis concerning the same,
   viz. that existence determines consciousness. I would contend
   that my formulation is to be preferred until a Marxist can
   demonstrate his provision for the world without using those
   Marxist terms for constituting it which unavoidably provide for
   it as that (Marxist) world.
7 It is important to see that the publicly available methods of
   science attach primarily to the presentation of findings and not
   necessarily to what goes on in the laboratory which might have
   an altogether different ad hoc character. This is brought out
   very clearly in Watson's (1968) account of the discovery of the
   structure of DNA, which contrasts the 'ad hocing' in the laboratory with the methodological formality of the published version
   of their findings.
8 Aaron Cicourel (1964) has extensively examined the problematic
   features of measurement in sociology.
9 The examples are taken from Kuhn (1970a).
10 The case of Watson and Crick is interesting for the way in which
   their work indicates the legitimacy and necessity of theorizing
   in the face of the counter claim that to do science is to engage
   in the painstaking work of examining strictly empirical data in
   the laboratory. During the time in which they were engaged upon
   their work on DNA they found themselves subject to stricture by
   fellow colleagues who operated with this view of science as en-
   gaging in 'hard' research. Objections were silenced, of course,
   when Watson and Crick produced their breakthrough. Some parallel is to be found in sociology, particularly with reference to
   the work of Parsons, which has been attacked for its strongly
   theoretical character. Yet it is precisely because Parsons insists on the necessity of a theoretic stance that his work remains more sophisticated than that of many of his critics despite its obvious deficiencies in the sense that he attends,

albeit in a limited way, to the problems of reflexivity whereas they do not.

11 Durkheim's own treatment of the phenomenon of suicide is instructive in this respect but the approach he advocates is a feature of most sociological explanations. See, for example, P.Filmer et al. (1972), for a discussion of positivistic sociology.

BIBLIOGRAPHY

BARBER, B. (1952), 'Science and the Social Order', New York, Free Press.
BLUM, A. and McHUGH, P. (1971), The Social Ascription of Motives, 'American Sociological Review', vol.36, no.1.
CICOUREL, A. (1964), 'Method and Measurement in Sociology', New York, Free Press.
DURKHEIM, E. (1938), 'The Rules of the Sociological Method', University of Chicago Press.
FILMER, P. et al. (1972), 'New Directions in Sociological Theory', Collier-Macmillan.
GARFINKEL, H. (1967), 'Studies in Ethnomethodology', Englewood Cliffs, N.J., Prentice-Hall.
HARRE, R. (1964), 'Matter and Method', Macmillan.
KUHN, T. (1970a), 'The Structure of Scientific Revolutions', University of Chicago Press.
KUHN, T. (1970b), Logic of Discovery or Psychology of Research, in I.Lakatos and A.Musgrove (eds), 'Criticism and the Growth of Knowledge', Cambridge University Press.
McHUGH, P. (1970), On the Failure of Positivism, in J.Douglas (ed.), 'Understanding Everyday Life', Routledge & Kegan Paul.
POPPER, K. (1959), 'The Logic of Scientific Discovery', Hutchinson.
WATSON, J.D. (1968), 'The Double Helix', New York, Atheneum.

Chapter 5

LITERARY STUDY AS LIBERAL EDUCATION AND AS SOCIOLOGY IN THE WORK OF F. R. LEAVIS

Paul Filmer

As our writings are, so are our feelings, and the finer the discrimination as to the value of those writings, the better chance
there is of not being ashamed of being a human being. Edgell
Rickwood (1933)

A literature which invites its audience to question the prevail-
ing social structure and social consciousness must constantly
question and expose itself. The power of language reassociates
itself with the perception of language ... Language and literature must revive their true identity - as the cutting edge of
perception. Creativity and the critical spirit must achieve a
new harmony and interdependence.
     ... new forms of alienation arise more rapidly than the old
ones are destroyed. Man, becoming himself less and less the
slave of nature, becomes the slave of counter-nature, which
springs from the applied science of nature. Scientific and
technological innovations outpace our capacity to absorb and
humanise them, with the terrible result that man is becoming increasingly alienated from his most distinctive faculty, his intelligence. At the same time the products of this intelligence,
knowledge and skill, drive him to fragment his personality, to
narrow specialisation, to the imitation of automata, to worship
efficiency and pay the price in soul-destroying boredom, to edu-
cate himself highly while increasingly delegating to elites his
participatory role in collective decision-making. David Caute
(1971)

There is a very current view in our world that philosophy should
be left to the philosophers, sociology to the sociologists, and
death to the dead. I believe this is one of the great heresies -
and tyrannies - of our time. I reject totally the view that in
matters of general concern (such as the meaning of life, the
nature of the good society, the limitation of the human con-
dition) only the specialist has the right to have opinions - and
then only in his own subject. 'Trespassers will be prosecuted'
signs have, thank goodness, become increasingly rare in our
countryside; but they still spring like mushrooms round the

high-walled estates of our literary and intellectual life. In
spite of all our achievements in technology we are, outside our
narrow professional fields, mentally one of the laziest and most
sheep-like ages that has ever existed ... The main reason
dissatisfaction haunts our century, as criticism haunted the
eighteenth and complacency the nineteenth, is precisely because
we are losing sight of our most fundamental human birthright:
to have a self-made opinion on all that concerns us.   John Fowles
(1964)

INTRODUCTION

This paper is constituted in addressing a number of issues, and is
available for reading in at least as many ways. It attempts, initially and explicitly, an exegetic account of F.R.Leavis's ideas on
the importance to contemporary British socio-cultural life of
English literature and its disciplined, critical study. Some parts
of this paper are extracted from a longer, on-going work which examines social aspects and implications of some works of recent
English literary criticism. Constitutive of such an examination is
a consideration of the implications for sociological thought of
those works, which may be found reflected in this paper.
    Leavis has been centrally involved for more than a decade in what
is known as the debate over 'two cultures'. Much of the heat of
controversy has now passed from it and, in conventional wisdom, the
laurels of victory belong to Leavis's initial antagonist, C.P.Snow.
Yet so much of Leavis's most recent writing has been in specific relation to this debate that his contributions to it become unavoidably an implicit concern of this paper. By attempting to explicate
Leavis's central, specific arguments in the controversy - that there
is, and can be, only one culture (in the sense, that is, in which
the term culture is typically employed by the debate's major contributors) - this paper may be seen as an implicit and peripheral
contribution to it, and one that challenges the current verdict upon
it.
    Disciplined, critical study of English literature is proposed by
Leavis as being of central importance in a modern liberal education.
Hence this paper is also concerned implicitly with issues of the
relative importance of sociology to such an education. In the
context of this volume, indeed, it may be read as a sociology of
Leavis's version of literary education. The grounds for such a
claim on its behalf rest upon the contention that any sociology, of
whatever particular substantive form of education, is constituted in
sociological examinations of the social characters of three systematic and constitutive features of all educations. That all educations have three such features rests, in turn, upon considering
educations as collaboratively creative, systematic introductions to,
and practices of, systematically organized corpuses of knowledge,
which corpuses are seen here as systematically interrelated with one
another. Education's three systematic, constitutive features may be
seen, then, as: first, systematic introductions to knowledge;
which knowledge, second, is constituted of systematically organized
corpuses. It is to these corpuses that education may be seen as

providing systematic introductions. They may be treated, third, as semi-autonomous, because their autonomy is limited in the degrees to which they are seen, also, as organized in systematic interrelations with one another.

Considered in this way, as providing for methodic ways of examining social characters of education's systematic features, sociology of education, like sociology of any collection of human processes and actions, is reflexive upon itself, in that way. in which sociology of education is education in sociology. Since this paper considers Leavis's version of literary education (as a set of proposals for central, constitutive practices of a 'liberal' education) from a 'sociological' perspective it is written also as an attempt implicitly to constitute proposals for a literary critical perspective (and education) in sociology. I have attempted, that is to say, in writing this paper to make the reflexivity of its (my) sociological perspective an interesting topic of what the perspective constitutes in its addresses. In making such an attempt, I have attempted also to account for systematic, interrelated features of Leavis's version of literary education in ways that recover and reveal the reflexivity of their social characters. That reflexivity is here proposed as being constituted dialectically; it exists, that is, not only in accountings of the social characters as reflecting, in many ways, upon versions (literary and educational, for example) of social life, but also in accounting for their reflectings as <u>reflectings back upon, and, thus, unavoidably constitutive changings</u> of, those versions of social life upon which they 'first' reflected. The systematic, interrelated features of Leavis's version of literary education that are considered in this paper are not, in other words, lent social characters in a simple way, through being addressed and accounted for from a sociological perspective. Rather, they are written constitutively into account as through and through social, in the <u>social</u> processes of constitutively and collaboratively constructing, organizing and sustaining thought that are writing/reading.

SOCIO-LITERARY THOUGHT AND SOCIO-CULTURAL CRISIS

There have long been traditions of written social thought (though they are neither exclusively nor predominantly professional sociological ones) for which an important focus of concern has been to recommend more or less concrete proposals for more or less radical reconceptualizations and/or reforms of English liberal and humanistic education at all levels. (1) The traditions, characterized variously - and invariably disparagingly - as romantic, Luddite, utopian and reactionary, have been concerned to question fundamentally some implications for human social life of material innovation and progress. Writers in such traditions frequently ground their arguments within contentions that imaginative works of literature provide evidences, in many ways, of unprecedented, deep and severe crisis in the social and cultural lives of members of modern human collectivities.

That such crisis occurs in human collectivities characterizable as modern invokes concrete features of it most explicitly as tied to

the advent of such social processes as: urbanization, industrial
mass production and technology, mass media of communications, socio-
occupational mobility, comprehensive education, etc. Sociological
versions of these processes, and of their constitutive relationships
to socio-cultural crisis, are collected and available as varieties
of concepts and theories of 'mass society' and 'mass culture'. (2)
The particular version of crisis that is focused upon here, however,
is apparently literary, and is presented as a formulation of re-
current concerns in the critical writings - literary, social and
educational - of F.R.Leavis.

It is characterized by what seems to Leavis to be an inexorable
chain of events, initiated by development of mechanized industrial
production, and finding its essence in employment of the machine as
the symbol of modern human civilization itself. Using machines
leads to co-ordination of machine industries into increasingly
large, mass-production manufacturing complexes, whose operation requires highly concentrated, mobile populations of workers: masses.
Masses are the human tragedies of machine-dominated civilization.
They are agglomerations of those-who-might-have-been-men, led away
from their potential humanity by comprehensive, popular education,
and thereafter courted, talked at and thought of as masses for the
spurious, alienated power they bestow in politics organized around
notions of universal adult suffrage which cheapen and coarsen themes
of democracy and equality. The 'drift of modern life' is summarized
as follows:

> On the one hand there is the enormous technical complexity of
> civilisation, a complexity that could be dealt with only by an
> answering efficiency of co-ordination - a co-operative concen-
> tration of knowledge, understanding and will (and 'understanding'
> means not merely a grasp of intricacies, but a perceptive wisdom
> about ends). On the other hand, the social and cultural disinte-
> gration that has accompanied the development of the inhumanly
> complex machinery is destroying what should have controlled the
> working. It is as if society, in so complicating and extending
> the machinery of organisation, had incurred a progressive debili-
> ty of consciousness and of the powers of co-ordination and
> control - had lost intelligence, meaning and moral purpose ...
> The complexities being what they are, the general drift has been
> technocratic, and the effective conception of the human ends to
> be served that accompanies a preoccupation with the smooth
> running of machinery tends to be a drastically simplified one.
> (1948, pp.22-3) (3)

More recently, Leavis has characterized such a version of modern
life as a 'Technologico-Benthamite Age', (4) but the issue remains:
'A general impoverishment of life - that is the threat that, ironically, accompanies the technological advance and the rising standard
of living; and we are all involved' (1972, p.87). And 'we are all
involved' because it is 'a general impoverishment of life' that
threatens, at the deepest levels of our common (social) existences.
The depths of those levels are plumbed by Leavis in his notion of
culture, which exists, beyond definition, as the living centre of
men's shared (social) lives. As such a centre, culture gives life
to dynamic relations between such crucial features of human
existences-in-common as: art (especially literature); an ef-

fective, educated public; organic community; social life;
standards of critical judgment; language; the individual; the
university. And though it exists beyond definition, (5) Leavis
writes often and at considerable length to constitute its centrality
in and for his own work. For example:

A language - apart from the conventional symbols for it - is
really there, it really exists in full actuality, only in individual users; it is there only as its idioms, phrases, words and
so on, with the meaning, intention, force in which their life resides, are uttered and meant by me (for example) and taken by
you. Do they then belong to the public world (you can't point to
them), or are they merely personal and private? We know that the
brisk 'either-or' doesn't meet the case.

And language, in the full sense, in the full concrete reality
that eludes the cognizance of any form of linguistic science,
does more than provide an analogue for a 'culture' in that full
sense which very much concerns us ... it is very largely the essential life of a culture. (1969, p.49)

LANGUAGE AND LITERATURE: 'THE SHAKESPEAREAN ADVANTAGE'

Language itself is clearly the core of Leavis's cultural centre, and
as such the fundament of men's shared lives. Such a culture

transcends the individual as the language he uses transcends
him ... the culture that has decayed with tradition ... is not
merely a matter of literary taste. The culture in question which
is not, indeed, identical with literary tradition but which will
hardly survive without it, is a sense of relative value and a
memory - such wisdom as constitutes the residuum of general experience. It lives on in individuals, but individuals can live
without it ... (1932, p.31)

The notion of culture that is grounded so deeply in language is
raised here, also, in a different form - alongside the special manifestation of language that is literature. Leavis offers it as 'not,
indeed, identical with literary tradition but which will hardly survive without it'.

Language and literature are realized throughout Leavis's work in
deep and dialectical interrelationships of literary and socio-
cultural traditions which analogize, illuminate and, ultimately, may
enrich each other and those comparable relationships between men
which constitute their socio-cultural collectivities:

The greatest works of English literature represent a collaborative creativity of a completeness that has been forgotten.
Shakespeare was able to leave the English language enriched,
suppled and changed for all who were to come after him because
of the actuality and potentiality of the language he started
with - the language created by the English people in their daily
lives and speech, which, by way of the church, were in touch with
a higher cultural heritage. He could be the great popular drama-
tist and, at the same time, our supreme intellectual poet. The
last, the ultimate, great writer to enjoy the Shakespearean ad-
vantage was Dickens; the conditions and the very sense of the
possibility have vanished. (1972, p.184) (6)

In as many ways as language evidences and records the development of
socio-cultural changes into crisis, so too does literature. (7) But
two of these ways are of particular concern to Leavis: first, the
completeness of collaborative creativity between great creative
writers and their known and familiar publics of 'common readers',
which constitutes the essence of English literary tradition, has
been forgotten. Second, and as a result of that amnesia, the
creation of such literature itself is threatened. Dickens was 'the
last, the ultimate, great writer to enjoy the Shakespearean ad-
vantage', and although the tradition has sustained literary
creativity through the major works of Eliot and Lawrence, their
works are already constitutive of crisis in the tradition in which
they are grounded. Leavis nominates no successors to them; their
works stand to and in 'the Great Tradition' as, perhaps, the last
evincings of its greatness. (8) Yet he proposes his own work rather
as a programme for its resurrection than as a requiem for its passing, despite persistent misinterpretations of it as the latter. (9)
For though the completeness of collaborative creativity that the
greatest works of English literature represent may have been forgotten, and thus is in danger of being lost, social hope remains,
for Leavis, because

> we still have the English language, and a language ... is more
> than an instrument of expression; it registers the consequences
> of many generations of creative response to living: implicit
> valuations, interpretive constructions, ordering moulds and
> frames, basic assumptions. (1972, p.184)

Language, in this version, on every occasion that men utilize it as
'an instrument of expression', can be, simultaneously, a social existence for them in their common socio-cultural inheritance and tradition - a tradition that may yet live as and through their
language. For to use language understood in this way is, in effect,
to be an actively inheriting member of the common cultural heritage
registered constitutively within it; and thus to practise 'an art
of living, involving codes developed in ages of continuous experience, of relations between man and man, and man and the environment
in its seasonal rhythm' (1932, pp.207-8).

LANGUAGE AND LITERATURE: COMMON AND MINORITY CULTURES

Language is constituted, in Leavis's writings about it, as itself a
popular, common, 'real culture shared by the people at large'
(1932), which carries 'such wisdom as constitutes the residuum of
the general experience'. Its fundamental standards and values are
expressed in its uses in 'the discerning appreciation of art and
literature' by 'the few (in any society) who are capable of unprompted first-hand judgement' and the larger minority 'capable of
endorsing such first-hand judgements by genuine personal response'.
These particular processes of appreciation, judgment and response
constitute, collaboratively and creatively, 'accepted valuations' of
literature and socio-cultural life. And they are, themselves,
constitutive features of a vivid language. They are 'a kind of
paper currency based upon a very small proportion of gold. To the
state of such a currency the possibilities of fine living at any

time bear a close relation' (1948, pp.143-4).

Literature is established, thus, as the finest expression of the highest potentials available for men in fundamental, experiential standards and values that have been developed over generations of their shared lives. It is a minority culture, and stands in relation to the common, popular culture that is embodied in language as testimony to collaborative, creative strivings of the latter's members towards truth. and a good life. It is the human, social beauty of those strivings, for, like language, it lives only as a meeting and sharing of the consciousness of men. It has the 'power of evoking contemporary reality so that it lives for us today' (1972, p.81).

LITERATURE AND CRITICISM: COLLABORATIVE CREATIVITY AS A MEETING OF MINDS

Literature can only re-evoke the contemporary reality about which it is written, according to Leavis, in and through the 'collaborative-creative process' that is criticism. For criticism constitutes literature's existence as something more than 'the black marks on the page' that may be the physical appearance of, for example, a poem. In 're-creative response of individual minds' to those marks, that poem becomes

> something in which minds can meet ... It gives us, too, the nature of English literature, a living whole that can have its life only in the living present, in the creative response of individuals, who collaboratively renew and perpetuate what they participate in - a cultural community or consciousness. (1972, p.62)

Literature's quintessential expression of the living culture of men that is their shared language, and its explication in criticism - men meeting and sharing their consciousnesses in language - may be seen, thus, as placing artists (creative writers of literature) and critics (their initial collaborators) in centrally important positions in any socio-cultural collectivity. That this is for the most part unrecognized in contemporary England - that, indeed, it is a proposition which is frequently dismissed as naively idealistic - is, for Leavis, a further symptom of the crisis of which he writes.

His notion of the centrality of artists' creative work may be found in I.A.Richards's contention that a creative writer is concerned in his work 'with the record and perpetuation of the experiences which seem to him most worth having ... he is also the man who is most likely to have experiences of value to record. He is the point at which the growth of the mind shows itself'. (10) Such a notion provides Leavis with grounds from which to contend, on behalf of Dickens (who serves here as an example for other writers in 'the Great Tradition'), that, since he was a great novelist, he was also

> an incomparable social historian. It is the great novelists above all who give us our social history; compared with what is done in their work - their creative work - the histories of the professional social historian seem empty and unenlightening. Dickens himself lived intensely, experienced intensely at first hand a wide range of the life of his time, and was peculiarly

well qualified to make the most of his opportunities of ob-
serving. His power of evoking contemporary reality so that it
lives for us today wasn't a mere matter of vividness in rendering
the surface; it went with the insight and intelligence of
genius. The vitality of his art was understanding ... He saw
how the diverse interplaying currents of life flowed strongly and
gathered force here, dwindled there from importance to relative
unimportance, settled there into something oppressively stagnant,
reasserted themselves elsewhere as strong new promise. The forty
years of his writing life were years of portentous change, and,
in the way only a great creative writer, sensitive to the full
actuality of contemporary life, could, he registers changing
England in the succession of his books with wonderful vividness.
(1972, pp.81-2)

Leavis accounts, in this passage, for the genius of Dickens's
creativity. But he has proposed literature as a collaborative-
creative process, and the passage itself exemplifies this collaborative work - the collaboration of critic with creative writer to
explicate the import of the latter's work as vivaciously constitutive of the language that sustains the processual, socio-cultural
life of (in this case) England. It is in this way that Leavis, as
critic, offers his 'first-hand judgement' as 'discerning appreciation' of Dickens's creative work, and encourages 'genuine personal
response' to it and to Dickens's work from his and Dickens's
readers. Thus, the minds of those readers (amongst whom you, reading this, and I may be collected) can meet in criticism of literature. For genuine personal response is formulated as a type of
judgment upon and valuations of that which is under consideration,
which constitutes

the 'third realm' - the collaboratively created human world, the
realm of what is neither public in the sense belonging to science
(it can't be weighed or tripped over or brought into the laboratory or pointed to) nor merely private and personal (consider the
nature of a language, of the language we can't do without ...
(1972, p.98)

THE 'THIRD REALM': LITERATURE'S CLAIM TO CONSTITUTE VERSIONS OF
SOCIO-CULTURAL LIFE

Leavis's work is a constitutive feature of the 'third realm'; it
takes place within it and it addresses it as a topic that incorporates, and to which are subordinate, all other topics in his work.
(The constitutive interrelationships of all these topics are set out
diagrammatically as Figure 1.) And it is in this concept of 'third
realm' that the social character of Leavis's concept of the collaborative-creative processes that are literature and its criticism may
be seen most clearly. For the 'third realm' is, above all, social -
what other sense and character attends a world characterized as
'collaboratively created' and 'human', as not a public phenomenon,
where public has a sense which is glossed as objective (something
that could be 'weighed', 'tripped over' or 'pointed to') and
context-free (something that could be 'brought into the laboratory'). It is a world, too, which is not 'merely private and

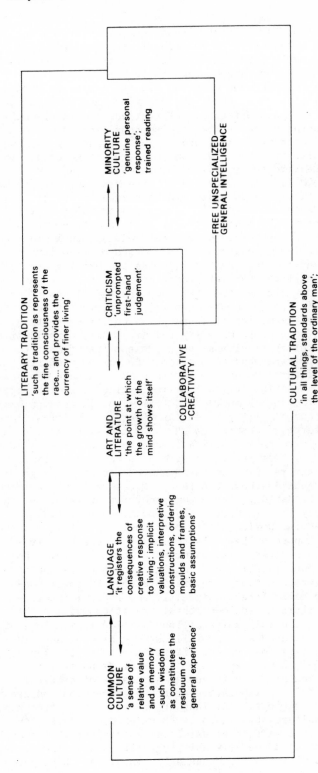

FIGURE 1   THE THIRD REALM   The collaboratively created human world, the realm of what is neither public ...
nor merely private –

personal', and Leavis characterizes it as such by reference to that
most remarkable of established social practices, language. (11)
Indeed, the 'third realm', in important senses, is language and its
myriad ramifications. For language exists in a mutually constitutive relationship with common culture, and the senses of words
themselves are relative valuings of the memories they carry of that
wisdom that 'constitutes the residuum of the general experience'.
In the words of language are written the supreme expressions of the
art of language's human use - literature; and in such expressions
the memories of collective human wisdom that are words become also
points in which creative human growth is proposed. That way of
living creatively in language, the way of literary art, (12) is responded to as creatively (and, again, in language) in the way that
is criticism, whose 'unprompted, first-hand judgement' sustains
literature's creativity by making it available, for 'genuine
personal response' through trained critical reading, to a wider con-
sociation of common language users - the members of minority
culture. Their uses of language, in teaching and writing, for example, return it, enriched through growth in creative human use, to
common culture - the culture, from its deep and fertile embeddedness
in which, its users (the culture's members) first drew it forth for
use. Such creative ex-cursion of language, from its generative
locus in common culture, into minority culture is its constitutive
utilization, as literary tradition, to represent 'the finer
consciousness of the race' and to provide 'the currency of finer
living'. (13) It returns to and re-enters common culture especially
enriched by the re-creation of its 'implicit valuations, interpretive constructions, ordering moulds and frames, basic assumptions'.
Re-creation is language's life, in and as literary tradition; and
that re-creation further constitutes the valuations, constructions,
moulds, frames and assumptions available as the senses-in-use of
language's words, in their return to common culture, as cultural
tradition. For their re-creation is an enrichment of language with,
'in all things, standards above the level of the ordinary man' and
thus, as cultural tradition, with a homogeneity that maintains 'a
surer taste than any that is merely individual can be'. (14)
    In the human, social world that is the 'third realm' is found a
key to the social import of Leavis's notion of a collaborative-
creative relationship between literature and its criticism. For
that relationship both requires and enables the perpetuation of
minority culture, whose members are distinguished by their possession of what he calls 'free, unspecialized, general intelligence'. Current crisis in socio-cultural traditions within the
'third realm' - one crucial manifestation of which is its loss of
homogeneity - has produced an especially strong need of such intelligence. It was its lost homogeneity that enabled its language
to return to common culture, enriched by re-creations of its
implicit values which had been forged as standards of critical
judgment through their collaborative-creative expression and use in
literature and its criticism. If language cannot return from minority to common culture, then each is threatened with disinte-
grative fission into a variety of unrelated specialisms. Language
is, literally, lost as a socially unifying, life-sustaining force,
for its commonness disappears increasingly rapidly as it proceeds

on its ex-cursions. Instead of being returned, as cultural tradition, to common culture from whence it was brought forth in use,
it is projected ever onwards in a crazy tide of jargon to fill the
shallow puddles of professional vocabularies. (15)

RECONSTITUTING A HUMAN VERSION OF SOCIO-CULTURAL LIFE: 'FREE, UN-
SPECIALIZED, GENERAL INTELLIGENCE' AS A RESPONSE TO SOCIO-CULTURAL
CRISIS

Leavis's notion of socio-cultural crisis, existing in such effects
of rapid, industrial social change as mechanization and specialization, constitutes such a destructive threat to socio-cultural traditions that 'there is a general recognition, helpless enough, of a
deep and frightening human disorder (the consequence, or concomitant, of change) that menaces civilisation itself' (1972, p.36). In
face of such a threat there are, theoretically, two possible responses: either to attempt to restore to common culture its lost
homogeneity; or to forge new means of sustaining the continuity of
its heritage, despite its increasing heterogeneity. They present
Leavis with no choice, however; only one response, the latter, is
possible. For to attempt to restore to common culture its lost
homogeneity would require actions akin to a new Luddism, which
Leavis does not advocate - despite persistent accusations against
him to the contrary. (16) That homogeneity was grounded, for
Leavis, in a mode of social organization that he has termed 'organic
community', (17) and which existed in such deep interrelationships
with it that to restore the former would unavoidably require an ac-
companying re-establishment of the latter - a goal which, for
Leavis, is impossible. The organic community has finally gone, 'not
to be restored in any foreseeable future'. The way of life by which
it manifested itself 'can't by any serious mind be proposed as an
ideal aim in our world' (1972, pp.85-6). It has been submerged in
the development of 'technologico-Benthamite civilization', which has
affected all features and processes of socio-cultural life:
    Mass production, standardization, levelling-down - these three
    terms convey succinctly what has happened. Machine-technique has
    produced change in the ways of life at such a rate that there has
    been something like a breach in cultural continuity; sanctions
    have decayed; and, in any case, the standards of mass-production
    (for mass-production conditions now govern the supply of litera-
    ture) are not those of tradition. Instead of conventional
    respect for traditional standards we have the term 'high-brow';
    indeed, such remains of critical standards as a desperate and
    scattered minority may now fight for can hardly be called tra-
    ditional, for the tradition has dissolved: the centre - Arnold's
    'centre of intelligent and urbane spirit', which, in spite of his
    plaints, we can see by comparison to have existed in his day -
    has vanished ...
        It is then vain to hope that standards will somehow re-
    establish themselves in the higgling of the market; the ma-
    chinery of civilisation works unceasingly to obliterate them.
    (1932, pp.137-8)
The citation of literature as a case to demonstrate the range and

depth of penetration into modern socio-cultural life of an ethos
manifesting itself as processes of 'mass-production, standardi-
zation, levelling-down' is crucial in the senses set out in the two
previous sections above. Once these processes invade literature and
its tradition, and begin to undermine the minority culture at its
centre, they begin also to make incursions which may be fatal into
socio-cultural grounds of human life itself. For human life's
socio-cultural character is grounded in ways in which men may share
and make common (in the finest sense) their experiences; that is,
in communication. The fundamental vehicles of communication are
languages, of all sorts; and of these the most highly developed,
sensitive and sophisticated - and thus the most fitting to the task
of conveying the wealth and complexities of human experiences between men - are verbal languages. They are developed to their
fitting sensitivities in and as collaboratively creative processes
of writing/reading literature and its criticism. And members of
minority culture, whose practices sustain these processes by return-
ing languages to common culture for all its members to use, enable
those members collaboratively to re-create and sustain their soci-
ality by sustaining their socio-cultural tradition. As Leavis
points out forcefully,

> A language is a life, and life involves change that is continual
> renewal. A language has its life in use - use that, of its
> nature, is a creative human response to changing conditions, so
> that in a living language we have a manifestation of continuous
> collaborative creativity. (1972, p.183)

To respond humanly and socially to socio-cultural crisis, then, is
to seek ways of saving language, and its important words, from re-
duction to 'cliché-use' and 'cliché-status'; for clichés

> have behind them clichés of attitude; expressions and inducers
> of flatteringly plausible non-thought, they make thought, unless
> in the way of recoil, protest and repudiation, impossible. The
> defence of humanity entails their reclamation for genuine
> thought. (1972, p.163)

Among the most important of words to be reclaimed are those upon
which may be focused some relevances of Leavis's work for sociology:
'individual' and 'social'. Central as they are to formulation of
any sociological argument, it is crucial that they should be used in
ways that would not empty them of life by sterilizing them, 'in the
technologico-Benthamite spirit, and cut them off from all vibration,
resonance or hint of the pregnant human truths and significances
they should be felt to portend' (1972, p.172). For Leavis, the relationship between the meanings potentially available in these two
words is no 'crude antithesis'; rather, a propos of Blake, he
points to it as an essentially collaborative-creative, and, thus,
social one:

> Except in the individual there is no creativity ... But the
> potently individual such as an artist is discovers, as he ex-
> plores his most intimate experience, how inescapably social he is
> in his very individuality ... He is ... a focal conduit of the
> life that is one, though it manifests itself only in the myriad
> individual beings, and his unique identity is not the less a
> unique identity because the discovery of what it means entails a
> profoundly inward participation in a cultural continuity - a con-

tinuous creative collaboration, something that must surely be
called 'social'.
　　'Identity' is Blake's word. He uses it in relation to
'selfhood', its antithesis. The individual as 'selfhood' wills
egoistically, from his own enclosed centre, and is implicitly
intent on asserting possession. As creative identity the individual is the agent of life, and 'knows he does not belong to
himself'. He serves something that is quite other than his
selfhood, which is blind and blank to it. (1972, pp.171-2)
The invocation of Blake here is essential. It is to Blake as an
exemplary creative writer, and to his implied reclamations of the
words 'individual' and 'social', that Leavis is referring. For
language can be saved only by men making themselves consciously
aware of its potential as a medium for expressive constitution of
the common, shared, human experiences that are socio-cultural life.
And creative explorations of that potential take place as literature, to which criticism, as collaborative-re-creative explications
of such explorations, bears a crucially important relationship.
Moreover, literature enables its readers, by its re-creative powers,
not only to see socio-cultural crisis as a threat; its very availability (in so far as that is limited by 'mass-production conditions') enables them to experience important features of the
crisis itself. Yet as long as literature and literary tradition are
still in existence, literature is available still as
　　a living whole that can have its life only in the living present,
　　in the creative response of individuals, who collaboratively
　　renew and perpetuate what they participate in - a cultural com-
　　munity or consciousness. (1969, p.172)
However, unless men undertake together,
　　by dint of sustained and intelligent purpose, the habit and means
　　of fostering in itself this collaborative and creative renewal,
　　the cultural consciousness and the power of response will fade
　　into nullity, and technological development, together with ad-
　　ministrative convenience, will impose the effective ends and
　　values of life, at the cost of an extreme human impoverish-
　　ment ... (1969, p.172)
The threat to literature is, thus, a threat to social life. And any
response to that latter threat has to be a response to literature,
for in studying it men can experience, collaboratively and re-
creatively, language's potential for expressing socially their
(individual) consciousnesses of their common, human membership of
'a cultural community or consciousness'. A central aim of response
to socio-cultural crisis has to be the ultimate re-establishing of
common culture, for anything less would be to abandon literature to
a position of marginal relevance to social life - a fate that, already, seriously threatens it.
　　Response is commenced, Leavis proposes, in systematic cultivation
of 'free, unspecialized, general intelligence'. Such intelligence
can only be developed in serious work that is constituted within a
culture in such a way that it is potentially available to any of its
members who are willing to undertake socially such creative human
efforts as its understanding requires - only in that way can its
free, unspecialized and general character be guaranteed. Literature
fulfils these requirements uniquely, for it is an expression of, and

in, common culture's universally available and fundamental vehicle
of communication: its language.

'Free, unspecialized, general intelligence' can have nothing to
do with the phenomenon constituted and measured by IQ scales. It is
a constitutive feature of the 'third realm', and as such cannot be
quantified, 'weighed' or 'brought into the laboratory'. Moreover,
its free, unspecialized and general character declares it as the
property of no specialism, and thus as not measurable in terms of
such qualifications as may certify professional competences in one.
Just as it cannot be formed by study of particular academic disciplines, so its application cannot be confined within any of their
boundaries. Above all, it is intelligence about human, social existence, about qualitative dimensions of experiences of socio-
cultural life; and thus it transcends academic classifications and
postulated, limiting relationships implied by particular discipli-
nary formulations of phenomena. Rather, it unites them all in a
considered attention to their relevances for socio-cultural life.
And to develop it in addressing literature is to undertake socio-
cultural practices in the two senses, which are, respectively, the
methods and the central aim of such address.

The methods are those of literary criticism and the central aim
is the creation of 'a strong and vital educated public'. Both require sustained, collaborative-creative human efforts towards
creation of human, social possibilities; and neither predicates
achievement of its goals in any final sense. Instead, and in each
case, such 'collaborative human creativity ... creates, and re-
creates, its sense of possible solutions, further problems, and
remoter goals as it goes on: its perception of problems and goals
changes' (1972, pp.186-7).

LITERARY CRITICISM AS A SOCIAL PRACTICE

To practise literary criticism is, in a disciplined, systematic way,
to read works of literature collaboratively and creatively with
others, in collaboratively re-creative relationships with their
writers. It is social in two senses, then: concretely, inasmuch as
it is a set of creative pratices, carried out collaboratively with
others; and symbolically, as an imaginative re-creation by readers
of the works of literature themselves - imaginatively rewriting them
in reading them, so to speak, and thus 'becoming' the others who are
the writers. Critical analysis of a poem, for example, according to
Leavis,

   is the process by which we seek to attain a complete reading of
   the poem - a reading that approaches as nearly as possible to the
   perfect reading. There is about it nothing in the nature of
   'murdering to dissect', and suggestions that it can be anything
   in the nature of a laboratory-method misrepresent it entirely.
   We can have the poem only by an inner kind of possession; it is
   'there' for analysis only so far as we are responding appropriately to the words on the page. In pointing to them (and there
   is nothing else to point to) what we are doing is to bring into
   sharp focus, in turn, this, that, and the other detail, juncture
   or relation in our total response; or (since 'sharp focus' may

be a misleading account of the kind of attention sometimes required), what we are doing is to dwell with a deliberate, considering responsiveness on this, that or the other node, or focal
point in the complete organisation that the poem is, in so far as
we have it. Analysis is not a dissection of something that is
already and passively there. What we call analysis is, of
course, a constructive and creative process. It is a more deliberate following-through of that process of creation in response to the poet's words that reading is. It is a re-creation
in which, by a considering attentiveness, we ensure a more than
ordinary faithfulness and completeness. (1948, pp.69-71)
The critic's responses to a work, once he has entered into, and provided that he can sustain, possession of it, further guarantee the
social character of his reading. For he expresses them as judgments
of value and of significance which 'place' the poem in the literary
and cultural traditions of the 'third realm', to which it is its
author's contribution and of which it is the guarantee of his
membership. They are judgments, that is, of the poem's value and
significance in re-creating, through the act of rewriting that is
reading it, the reader/(re-)writer's sense of his membership of
those traditions, and thus, ultimately, of the common culture that
they feed, and by which they are fed. The social character of
critical practices for Leavis is evoked most strongly when he speaks
of his effort as a critic having been 'to work in terms of concrete
judgements and particular analyses: "This - doesn't it? - bears
such a relation to that; this kind of thing - don't you find it
so? - wears better than that," etc.' (1966, p.215). By these
methods the 'unprompted first-hand judgements' that are 'the discerning appreciation of art and literature' by the 'few (in any society)' capable of making them are formulated, and are endorsed by
'genuine personal response' of a 'larger minority'. Such collaborative re-creation is clearly a specialized discipline of study,
practised by members of minority culture. And while it may sustain
the continuous re-creation of 'free, unspecialized, general intelligence', it cannot, as a specialism, return the language that it has
regenerated and enriched to common culture. Yet without doing so,
it cannot adequately contribute to the sustaining of cultural continuity, for which purpose Leavis sees 'a strong, vital and educated
public' as especially important. As a solution to this problem,
then, the importance of Leavis's notion of such a public may be addressed explicitly, together with its close and indispensable interrelationships with disciplined, but non-specialist, literary study.

NON-SPECIALIST LITERARY STUDY AND A STRONG, VITAL AND EDUCATED
PUBLIC

In the creation of 'a strong, vital and educated public', Leavis
sees as coming together all the features of human socio-cultural
life that he regards as crucial to the continuation and regeneration
of common culture. (Figure 2 attempts to set out diagrammatically a
view of collaborative-creative relationships between these
features.) It is possessed, particularly, of 'free, unspecialized,
general intelligence' developed in collaborative-creative study of

literature. Such study is conducted by members of a university, in
what Leavis calls its English school, but for the sake of neither
the university nor literature, but rather for the sake of social
life, in the special senses outlined above. Leavis points out
explicitly that:

> The university as I contend for it is not an ultimate human goal;
> it is the answer to a present extremely urgent need of civili-
> zation. The need is to find a way to save cultural continuity,
> that continuous collaborative renewal which keeps the 'heritage'
> of perception, judgement, responsibility and spiritual awareness
> alive, responsive to change, and authoritative to guidance. In
> that continuity inhere the 'ahnung' and the nisus that, ef-
> fectively energizing the few, represent humanity's chance of es-
> caping the disasters from which scientists, technologists and
> economists, as such and alone, cannot save us. For not only
> faith, but creativity in the realm of the spirit, the realm of
> human significances, is necessary ... It is in and of the situ-
> ation not only of a Blake but of humanity (in the personal foci
> that represent it) that the problem of the 'telos', the ultimate
> goal, being in question, the nisus can never achieve the final
> satisfaction and the supersession of the 'ahnung'; what it can
> hope to achieve is the advance that brings a fresh field of data
> into view and establishes a new situation for insight to work on.
> (1972, p.27)

Whatever the detailed methods, if any at all, of whichever way may
be chosen collectively to save cultural continuity, Leavis's work
leaves no doubt of the focus of attention of those methods.
Language, and its supremely creative expression in literature,
demands pre-eminent attention as the fundamental vehicle of cultural
tradition. And it is for this reason that non-specialist study of
literature, in university English schools, is proposed as the locus
of development of free, unspecialized, general intelligence:

> The essential discipline of an English school is the literary-
> critical; it is a true discipline, only in an English school if
> anywhere will it be fostered, and it is irreplaceable. It
> trains, in a way no other discipline can, intelligence and sensi-
> bility together, cultivating a sensitiveness and precision of re-
> sponse and a delicate integrity of intelligence - intelligence
> that integrates as well as analyses and must have pertinacity and
> staying power as well as delicacy ... The kind of work advocated
> entails, in its irreplaceable discipline, a most independent and
> responsible exercise of intelligence and judgement on the part of
> the student. The more advanced the work, the more unmistakably
> is the judgement that is concerned inseparable from that pro-
> foundest sense of relative value which determines, or should
> determine, the important choices of actual life ... the literary
> critical discipline ... can, in its peculiar preoccupation with
> the concrete, provide an incomparably inward and subtle initi-
> ation into the nature and significance of tradition. (1948, pp.
> 34-5) (18)

Language, moreover, is of fundamental importance to all disciplines, whether specialist or general - and especially to social
life itself ('a language is a life') - for without it the communication that both makes specialization possible and yet restrains it

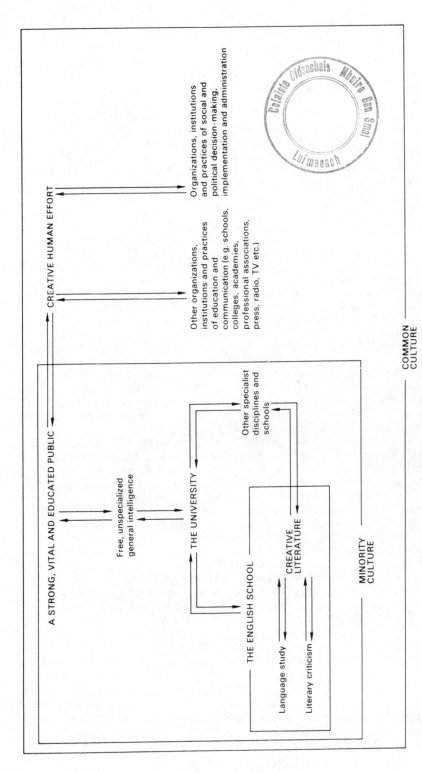

FIGURE 2   Collaborative-creative relationships between literature the university and common culture

from human, social irrelevance would not be possible. Specialist
disciplines and practices sustain their human, social relevance by
their practitioners' communications with one another, and with still
others who practise no specialisms. Those communications are human
and social practices, whether carried out as constitutive, in part,
of specialist disciplines or not. And while such communications
may be sustained to posit and proselytize for two cultures - whatever euphemisms are preferred for them: science and technology
versus arts and humanities; specialist as against general or
liberal - to do so, Leavis suggests, is 'a dangerous form of unin-
telligence' (1969, p.177). There is, in this sense, only one
culture: the common culture that unites within it all specialisms
and minority cultures through the language that members and practitioners of them all use in common. Common culture is the source
from which the languages of specializations are drawn and to which,
finally, they must be returned if the specialist practices in which
language is employed are to have any positive human and social
significance. By human linguistic communication the import of
specialist studies, experiments and researches are returned, socially, to those upon whose behalf they are conducted, and who must
decide upon their human, social worth. Furthermore, much of that
worth is conveyed, since language is a major vehicle of cultural
continuity, in the language chosen by specialists to communicate to
others the import of their work. Sensitivity to language - to
choice and sequencing of words - is in this sense sensitivity also,
and crucially to human, social membership of common culture as a
humanly social way of living. Attending to the presence or absence
of such sensitivity - and responding to this presence - amounts to
a concern to guard against the descent of language and its important
words into 'cliché-status' and 'cliché-use', and has the same implications for thought (see above, p.66).

Thus, the 'fresh field of data' that is brought into view by non-
specialist literary education, and the 'new situation for insight to
work on' for which it provides a central occasion, is language
itself as an axiomatic means of human, and humane, communication,
and as a crucial indicator of its users' sensitivities to membership
of common culture as a humanly social way of living. Language is
studied in its most exploratory and creative uses - as literature.
In such forms of use it explores and creates possibilities and potentials not only for itself, but also - because of its character as
a human vehicle of communication - for social life. Indeed, for
Leavis, processes of collaborative-creative study that constitute
trained reading ('a reading that approaches as nearly as possible
the perfect reading') of literature represent a microcosm of developing potentials of humane, social relationships in common
culture. Yet they do so in a sense that limits them in no way to
the form of a blueprint, or fixed plan, for social life.

Such non-specialist study of language, through collaborative-
creative, critical studies of literature, is seen by Leavis as oc-
curring in active, fertile, on-going interrelationships with studies
in other specialist disciplines to produce free, unspecialized,
general intelligence. The institutional setting of such production
is the university, as Leavis contends for it, in whose English
school the small, judging minority of the few whose ability to make

genuine, first-hand judgments of the relative value of literary art
initiates the necessary critical study collaboratively-creatively
with members of the larger, responding minority who are able to en-
dorse their judgments with genuine, personal response (see above,
pp.60-1,69). Members of the responding minority are drawn not only
from the English school but from other specialist disciplines and
schools as well, and thus constitute the university as a whole as
central agent in constituting a 'humane centre' of free, unspecialized, general intelligence at the heart of a strong, vital, educated
public. (19) Only in a public so constituted, Leavis argues, could
cultural continuity be sustained (20) - continuity, that is, of
common culture. Yet this appears to be a paradox: continuity of
common culture is here being proposed as able to be safeguarded only
by a succession of minorities. First, the active work of safeguarding is located in minority groups (English schools) of minority
organizations (universities). Second, within English schools, two
minorities - the judging minority and the responding minority - do
the safeguarding work in creative collaboration, thereby educating
the larger minority to enter the public, and to live actively within
it, as its vital, humane, intelligent centre. How can a common
culture be safeguarded by a succession of minorities, even the totality of whose members are in no way coterminous with, nor claim
representativeness of, the members of that common culture?

Resolutions of the paradox are found in Leavis's work in two
distinct ways: first, in the central, analogical importance of
language to the existence, and thus to understandings, of culture.
Leavis constitutes culture in a collection of organically interrelated and interdependent ways of living; it is a residuum of
general experience, laid down by and sustained in the mutually
other-directed and interrelated social practices of successive
generations of its members. The experiences of social ways of
living that it embodies involve codes of value, standards - both
prescriptive and judgmental - that are developed from, and thus
available as, practices of members of the culture. (Recognition of
them, indeed, and ability to undertake them, may be seen as a
guarantee of membership.) Such practices provide for continuance
of social characters of culture's ways of living; and those that
come closest to concrete manifestations of culture exist in, and are
communicated within and between generations and groups of members
by, language. It is in this sense that 'a language is a life', for
within it lives the invaluable residuum of general, time-transcend-
ing experiences of human, social life in a culture, laid down by
successive generations of its members, and available there for
generations of them to come.

A part of the residuum - in English culture, by Leavis's arguments, a most important one - lives in (English) literature. For
language has a life of its own, and is only turned to use by members
of a culture as a vehicle for communicating (as 'transmitting' and
'receiving', for using language is writing/reading, speaking/hear-
ing) their cultural heritage according to their sensitivities to
language's potential autonomy. (21) To say that language has a potential autonomy is to point here to its dialectical character in
use. Since it is written/read, spoken/heard, it is available to its
users, on every single occasion (such as throughout this paper now

being written/read) on which it is used, to communicate ideas,
beliefs, arguments, truths, falsehoods, etc., as at least two actually (and not potentially: potentially it must be infinitely more)
available sets of meanings - not only that which is written, but
that, also, which is read. Language, to understate the point, has
possibilities in use of which its users cannot possibly be aware.
And yet one generic, practical art of language use, collaborative-
creative writing/critical-reading of literature, is constituted in
an explicit concern with, and sensibility towards language's possibilities. Literature is the exploration of those possibilities, and
that exploration is, too, creation of language's possibilities.
For literature is the work of men, using language; thus, what
possibilities that work may show language as possessing are possibilities created by men. And as in literature, so in life. Men,
creating possibilities in language as literature, are creating
possibilities in life too; for 'a language is a life'. It is the
crucial role of the judging minority in university English schools
to examine literature for its creation of possibilities in language,
and thus in life; and for the larger, responding minority to ampli-
fy that response, by their vital uses of language, into a revivifi-
cation of the possibilities of life in common culture, of which both
minorities are members. This is the non-specialist work constitutive of their memberships, every bit as much as whatever may be
the work of their specialisms. Leavis adds emphasis to this point
by saying that he is

> not in the least tempted to think of English as the evangelizing
> presence among lesser breeds who must be taught the way to sal-
> vation. A strong and vital educated public represents a living
> cultural continuity, and that manifests itself, if it effectively
> does, in the responsiveness of a charged human maturity to the
> problems our world confronts us with. Obviously, in the gener-
> ation and renewal of this at the university, the creative centre,
> specialist disciplines and specialist branches of knowledge have
> their indispensable positive parts to play. (1972, p.186)

Thus, though the members of the judging and responding minorities
do not constitute common culture in its entirety, they are nevertheless and in a profound way of that culture. They exist, in English
schools, at the centres of universities, and so constitute 'the
creative centre' of cultural continuity for Leavis. In such a position, and because of the very special character of their (even
non-specialist) work, they cannot but be minorities, (22) according
to Leavis's essentially conservative view of English society. (23)
Thus he does not see their members as unrepresentative (in a con-
servative-democratic, perhaps Burkean sense of representative) of
common culture:

> The educated public, even when it is called the educated class
> ... couldn't possibly be called an oligarchy, and, for all the
> hazy incitement of 'elitism', it should be obviously absurd to
> call it 'an élite'. It isn't a class, either, in the politico-
> economic sense commonly attached to that word - the sense that,
> reducing 'social' in the Benthamite and post-Marxist way, defines
> 'class' in terms of the 'materialist' interpretation of human
> history. The educated class or public, intelligently conceived,
> comprehends people of widely varied social position, economic

self-interest and political standing - standing (that is) in
relation to the possibilities of political influence. Its importance, in fact, is conditioned by its diversity of presumable
bent and its lack of anything like ideological unity. When, as
may happen, it is moved to indignation, protest and resistance by
one of those casual threats to human life which characterize our
age of accelerating progress, that response tells because it so
clearly transcends sectional interest or bias ... The human
problem is complex and multiform: élites and oligarchies - and
great men too - are necessary, but so is that which can check,
control and use them, and, except as such a public, it can't
exist - there is no other conceivable presence. (1972, pp.213-14)
The 'complex and multiform' character of 'the human problem' that is
contemporary crisis in common culture for Leavis can be responded
to, in his view, by the kind of intense and sustained creative
effort that only minorities seem capable of producing. Creative
effort, he claims, starts from a 'general truth' that

there are no easy or evident solutions. For disinterested intelligence and the creative impulse that goes with it the urgency
of the human crisis is both a challenge and an opportunity; and
it is a further truth that their work is never conceived, and so
never initiated, by majorities. Democracy (if 'democracy' is to
be a good word) won't function unless the community has a strong
educated nucleus. I have spoken of the universities as the
creative centres of the educated public we need, and now, when
the idea of 'university' has been disembarrassed of the 'di-
visive' associations of the word 'class' in its political use,
is the moment to justify and enforce that emphasis by getting its
significance manifested to the utmost in evident fact. To say
this, of course, is not to do anything but honour the truth that
the university, if it is to have roots, can have them only in the
community - that it is society's necessary organ. And the
plainer it becomes that the supporting and fostering public it
depends on in its performance of its social function is a robust
reality the better, for the function can't be performed without
the evocation of hostilities and jealousies both insidious and,
in brutal ways, formidable. That is the sickness of our technologico-Benthamite civilization.
    For this ... is the century of the common man. And if the
profounder needs of the common man don't find, to serve them,
uncommonness more broadly based and enduring than a Churchill or
a de Gaulle the common man's future won't be anything to look
forward to. There must, then, be an educated public that
commands recognition as an impressive reality - as it will not do
if it is not confidently aware of its influence and of its responsibility. But a public that isn't conscious of itself as a
public, that doesn't know that it exists as such, is hardly one.
(1972, pp.215-6)
Leavis's second way of solving the paradox of safeguarding the
continuity of common culture in the works of a succession of minorities may be seen here as residing in his understanding and interpretation of the commonness of common culture as 'uncommonness ...
broadly based' which can serve 'the profounder needs' of the common
man. Such uncommonness, which is nevertheless broadly based, would

evidently be found only among minorities which could be of common
culture only as far as they would not, as Leavis proposes, separate
themselves from it by constituting and sustaining themselves as
oligarchies or élites. 'Common' men of common culture, as and
because of the commonness of their culture itself, are anything but
common in pejorative senses of that word.

Moreover, there is a second uncommonness about Leavis's use of
common in his characterization of common culture: it does not
connote a sense (even, presumably, in the phrase 'common sense') of
unanimity, of sense- or views-held-in-common by common culture's
members - and most especially not by members of the educated public:

What must be thought of as characterizing such a public is not
unanimity; one has rather ... to make the analogy of a language.
There will be enough in common in the way of basic values and
assumptions and deep implicit nisus to make differences that look
extreme the concomitant, or necessary manifestations, of a total
collaborative life. (1972, p.227)

These 'differences that look extreme' among members of the educated
public are what make it vital. And in as much as they do not
destroy it, they manifest the public's strength, for, though they
look extreme, they are 'the concomitant, or necessary manifestations, of a total collaborative life'; what Leavis has also
called 'creative quarrelling'. Such quarrelling would not be mean
or petty: the members of the public, in their indispensability,
represent for Leavis - especially in relation to art, but therefore
also in relation to language and to human socio-cultural life in
general - not only 'the effective presence of "standards"', but also
'the ability to modify, in response to significant creation, the
implicit criteria by which it (the public) judges' (1972, p.217).

The role of a strong, vital, educated public in Leavis's proposed
solution to socio-cultural crisis, then, is that of undertaking and
sustaining creative human effort, by creating and exploring possibilities of and for that effort. Its members have in common with
one another, and with their fellow-members of common culture, of
which they are its creative centre, a common language. Their
collaborative-creative studies of language's most exploratory and
creative expressions, literature, have made them conscious of the
wealth of potential of language itself, and of what language
carries: their cultural heritage. And thus they may be poised, in
undertaking creative human effort, to reveal to their fellow-members
of common culture the potential for creative living that their
common culture provides, and to do so, above all, by preventing the
erosion of that potential that is threatened by increasingly rapid
social change. The public's 'function would be to keep reforming
political and administrative activity from blindness and indiffer-
ence to any but short-term ends' (1969, p.179). The educated
public's creative human effort, in terms of practical action, lies
in influencing all members of common culture, through organizations
and institutions of education and communication, of social and political decision-making and administration, to the end of safeguarding that culture against disintegration in its crisis.

Thus the public in its totality will represent that strong living
sense of complexities which is needed, above all in a time of
rapid change, to ensure that the achievements, spiritual and

humane - the essential creative achievements - of our civilization shall be permanent gains, conserved in the cultural
heritage. (1972, p.227)

IN CONCLUSION: COLLABORATIVE-CREATIVE CRITICAL STUDY OF LITERATURE
AS AN IMPORTANT SOCIOLOGY

Because of the social and common cultural importance of literary
tradition, Leavis's arguments constitute a claim that it alone is
adequate to fulfil the requirements of a central core of topics for
study in the course of a humane, liberal education. Yet this
central place is contemporarily afforded more often, and more
readily, to the so-called social sciences. For Leavis, however, the
latter disciplines are crucially limited, in comparison with literary study, as ways of studying 'society, human nature and human
possibilities' by what he has termed 'the Benthamite calculus, the
statistical or Blue Book approach, and the utilitarian ethos' (1969,
pp.176-7). More explicitly,
    sociology and economics, if they are to be sciences, can give no
    adequate answer to the questions that are waived by that phrase
    'the standard of living' as the economists use it. Our problems
    cannot be settled without reference to the ends of life, without
    decisions as to what kind of life is desirable, and it is an
    elementary fallacy to suppose that such decisions can be left to
    science. But 'humane letters', though they may have no authority
    in the province of 'certified facts', have a good deal of
    authority in the question of what, in the long run, humanity is
    likely to find a satisfactory way of life. (1932, p.31)
    So much, perhaps, for sociology (and economics). Yet I want, by
way of a conclusion that may beg more problems than it resolves (not
without point, though, if it promotes creative quarrelling among
sociologists), to attempt to write into focus grounds for considering collaborative-creative critical study of literature as an
important sociology. (24)
    1 'An' important sociology, because Leavis's bald invocation of
sociology-with-no-article (and together with economics, as if both
were equally representative of the 'social sciences' as a whole),
carries with it implications for sociology that it is one unitary
and unified discipline (and that both sociology and economics conceive of men in similar ways). There is not one (or the) sociology;
there are several (and, for the most part, their practitioners conceive of men in considerably more human, less mechanistic ways than
do those of economics).
    2 An 'important' sociology, for reasons that I have tried, at
least implicitly, to set forth in all preceding sections of this
paper and which, therefore, I will not reiterate yet again, except
to quote Leavis once more that 'a language is a life' and, what is
more, a social life, which finds its most creative expression in
literature.
    3 And finally, an important 'sociology', because literary criti-
cism (collaborative-creative critical study of literature) is a
collection of unavoidably social practices, socially practised. It
is as inquiring into manifestations of the social, whether or not

they do so socially, (25) that sociologists consider themselves
properly and professionally engaged.

To characterize sociologists' proper and professional practices
as those of inquiring into the social may appear, even if true, to
be obvious and trivial. Yet such obviousness and triviality disappear rather disconcertingly upon considering the contention that
there is no such phenomenon as the social; only versions of it.
Considering the phenomenon 'social' in this way (that is, in its
versions) ceases to allow any longer avoidance of a central issue
in characterizations of social - the issue, that is, that may be
posed as the question: Which versions of social do practitioners
of professional sociologies study, as opposed to professional practitioners of versions of other disciplines which may also be characterized as involving study of versions of social? (26)

A sociology, like any other 'logos', is constituted by its practitioners in the distinctive and organized methods by which they
constitute and account for their inquiries into, and studies of its
distinctive topics. Such a (self-) constitution of any sociology is
a constitution of it as an unavoidably (if, to its professional
practitioners, for the most part an uninterestingly (27) 'reflexive'
sociology, for it both is and says what its professional practitioners inquire into and study. It is, that is to say, a collection of
distinctive methods for inquiries into and studies of its topics,
inasmuch as those methods are distinctive in their relationships
(which are of study) to the topics for whose study they provide.
The methods are appropriate to - they 'fit' and 'match' - the topics
for which they enable sociological inquiries. Yet appropriateness
of methods to topics is no natural or social coincidence, of neither
cosmic nor human dimensions: it is no coincidence at all, for professional sociologists characterize the topics of their sociologies
for themselves and for one another. And they do so by the very
methods with which they undertake inquiries into these topics. Professional sociologies' topics are as distinctive, to closely similar
degrees and in closely similar ways, as their methods; and this is
so because of their methods. In what has been called the sociological tradition, (28) major contributors to it have focused, equally
and teleologically, on both method(s) and topics. This point, too,
may read as obvious and trivial, unless and until (I write that)
we recall the enormous constraints under which professional sociologists place themselves when they use the explicatory analogy -
crucially important to the professional traditions of many sociologies (29) - of sociological methods with those of natural and physical sciences. Such constraints are relevant here in so far as they
require of professional sociologists that they constitute their
topics in unified and interrelated ways (e.g. as 'natural' phenomena
of social life, society, social interaction, etc.) which will befit
inquiries into them according to methods of 'the natural' science of
society that (in this sense, scientific) sociologies may be proposed
as being by their professional practitioners. Under such constraints, it is no longer a feature of any sociology that its practitioners, whether lay or professional, constitute its own methods
and topics (and thus its availability to practitioners of other
disciplines) in deep and mutually reciprocal interrelatedness.
Rather, its topics are presented as 'the natural' phenomena that are

the social; and its methods as the (as-if-universally established, and held) logical practices that are (professional, scientific) sociological investigation. (30)

In so characterizing its own topics for itself, any sociology makes itself contingent upon its own version of social. What is the social is no certainty, but a possibility, and one that is collaboratively and creatively produced by men and recognized as being of men, in the human mutuality of activities that manifest men's shared ways of being-together in (social) worlds.

According to these proposals for realizing sociologies as their practitioners' constitutings of sets of methodic practices addressing appropriate social topics, Leavis's work may be read - in its attempts to redefine and refine collaborative-creative critical study of literature as a self-consciously human, social and socially relevant practice - as a set of practices that constitute themselves into a sociology. The practices are clearly methodic, according to the negotiable criteria of methods by and with which literary critics work, in Leavis's conception of their work. And the on-going negotiability of those criteria, as a constitutive feature of criticism itself, guarantees that they are social ('This - doesn't it? - bears such a relation to that; this kind of thing - don't you find it so? - wears better than that, etc.'). Leavis's work has been, by his own account, in terms of such 'conrete judgements and particular analyses', and it has been conducted upon topics that are constituted in versions that emphasize their pre-eminently social dimensions. Its primary topic, literature, is important as art because it constitutes, in being written/read, men's most creative expressions and explorations of the potentials and possibilities of their shared language-in-use, as a fundamentally important vehicle for communication of their mutual humanity. Such exploration of language's potentials in art fits it for the task of enabling men socially to create, and creatively to communicate the possibilities of their shared, social ways of living. To engender such awareness of language's important social role, actual and potential, is for Leavis the work of humane, liberal education. To achieve it, he would place non-specialist, collaborative-creative critical study of literature as the centre of such education. And because of language's importance to social life as a whole, for which its imaginative social exploration in literary art is a crucial proving-ground, non-specialist literary criticism moves, rapidly and far, beyond literature itself for its topics. They cannot but encompass, finally, the whole of social life itself, in all its myriad human ramifications.

This paper attempts, in its writing, an account of Leavis's reconceptualizations of what it must have been, and might yet again become, for men to live intelligently, socially and humanely together. It attempts also to account for his notions of the grounds and methodic practices of a collaboratively-creative, disciplined, liberal education that might make possible understandings and practisings of such ways of being-socially in modern England. A tendency, among professional practitioners of established and 'scientific' sociologies, may be to ignore Leavis's ideas, or else

to refute them crudely as 'unscientific', 'unsociological',
'Luddite' or 'reactionary'. If they should do so, however, they may
court slow, distracted and lonely abandonings of life-that-could-
yet-become-true, because truly social. Such practices are not
strange to sociologists, yet they are nevertheless disastrous for
humanity. Parched by the glittering heat of science's deceptive
sun, in an intellectual desert of the arrogant certainty of so much
'scientific' sociological work - alienated, even, from ourselves -
we may wither in auto-destructive orgies of triumphant and positivist individualism.

NOTES

1 E.g. Leavis (1948, 1969, 1972); Williams (1961); Bantock
   (1963); Leavis and Thompson (1933); Thompson (1964).
2 E.g. Bell (1960); Bramson (1960); Kornhauser (1960); Lynd and
   Lynd (1956); McQuail (1969); Rosenberg and White (1958, 1970);
   Bensman and Vidich (1958), etc.
3 This passage was written in 1943, yet the issues it addresses
   were formulated at least ten years earlier in, e.g. Leavis and
   Thompson (1933). They are concerns to which he has consistently
   returned (see especially, (1969, 1972)). A more detailed
   attempt to formulate Leavis's socio-cultural life is made in
   Filmer (1969), especially pp.273-81.
4 See especially Leavis (1969, 1972). Some illuminating earlier
   comments on Bentham are to be found in Leavis's (1950) introduction to 'Mill on Bentham and Coleridge'.
5 'In our time it is very necessary to insist that the most
   important words - important for those troubled about the
   prospect that confronts humanity - are incapable of definition.
   You can't by defining them fix and circumscribe their life - for
   in any vital use they will live, even disconcertingly: there
   lies their importance for thought' (1972, p.163). Raymond
   Williams has also taken issue with legislative definitions of
   important words, and in related ways. See Williams (1958, pp.
   13-19 and 1973).
6 See also Leavis (1972, pp.81-3; 1969, pp.174-9; Leavis and
   Leavis, 1970, passim). For another, yet cognate, valuing of
   Dickens in this respect, see Marcus (1972), especially pp.196-
   200.
7 See here also Williams's different, though related, addressings
   of cultural change through language (1958; 1973). A very tentative, and brief, consideration of some relationships between
   Leavis's and Williams's respective enterprises is attempted in
   Filmer (1969), especially pp.280-91. Williams's work is also
   considered briefly in its consideration of language's ways of
   evidencing socio-cultural changes in Sandywell, Silverman,
   Roche, Filmer and Phillipson (1975).
8 On Eliot, see e.g. Leavis (1969), especially II, III, IV; on
   Lawrence, see especially Leavis (1955), and on 'the Great Tradition', see Leavis (1948).
9 Leavis refers to a variety of such misinterpretations, as interesting occasions for his self-explication, throughout his more
   recent work - see, for example, (1972), especially II and III.

10 Quoted in Leavis (1948, p.144). A brief account by Leavis of
the importance of Richards's early work in the development of
his own thinking is in (1969, pp.16-19).
11 Interesting professional sociological considerations of language
in this sense may be found, for example, in Berger and Berger
(1970), and Cicourel (1973).
12 Eliot's essay, Tradition and the Individual Talent, offers a
succinct version of the essentials of this way of living
creatively in language, and one which is important for an understanding of Leavis's conception of it. See Eliot (1920, pp.47-
59).
13 See Leavis (1932, p.208). Their context makes it clear that the
use of the word 'race' in these sequences refers to human,
cultural, and not genetic, inheritance.
14 Leavis (1932, pp.145-6).
15 The irony of writing these words as a professional sociologist,
for publication in a collection on sociology of education, does
not escape me. I hope that its recognition may help to free us
from some of the inhuman consequences of such irony.
16 Notably by Snow and Annan. The principal writings in Leavis's
debate with them are collected in the following: Annan (1966,
1970); Snow (1969, 1970); Leavis (1972).
17 Leavis explicates this phenomenon in various of his writings;
but see especially (1972, pp.84-6) and the Introduction to
Leavis and Thompson (1933). It depends upon the writings of
George Sturt, who wrote under the pen name of George Bourne
(1912, 1923). An account of Leavis's explications may be found
in Filmer (1969, pp.275-7, 279-80). Other corroborative sources
employed by Leavis are cited in Leavis (1972, pp.193-8).
18 This does not exclude, for Leavis, the importance of other
specialist disciplines. Just as 'scientists, technologists and
economists alone cannot save us' from the disasters threatened
by present socio-cultural crisis, similarly, literary-critical
education by itself could not be enough. Yet this is not
problematic, since 'one of the virtues of literary studies is
that they lead constantly outside themselves, and, on the other
hand, while it is necessary that they should be controlled by a
concern for the essential discipline, such a concern, if it is
adequate, counts on associated work in other fields. In fact,
for those who are seriously interested in it the problem
becomes, in an inevitable way ... that of devising an education
such as may properly be called liberal' (1948, pp.35-6).
Elsewhere, and more recently, Leavis has noted again, and
exemplified the importance of a co-presence of other specialist
disciplines with 'English schools' in universities (see, for example, 1972, pp.202-3, 217).
19 Leavis expands the concept of 'centre' as 'a field of study
existing as such by reason of a distinctive discipline of intelligence that it cultivates - a discipline sui generis that is
special though not specialist ...'. However, it is still to be
strived for in hope, for he goes on to remark that 'The inquiry,
pushed home, as to how far any actual English school fulfilled
this requirement would compel a recognition humiliating for us
who care' (1972, p.203).

20   The mutually constitutive relationship between collaborative-
     creative, critical study of literature and an educated public is
     suggested by Leavis as follows: 'The educated public, where
     there is one, is the effective presence of cultural continuity;
     English literature ... is a focal manifestation of the conti-
     nuity, and a lively general awareness of that truth - a due
     realisation of its significance - will be expressed in and
     fostered by a lively genuine performance of the function of
     criticism in and of our time' (1972, pp.220-1).

21   To compound the paradox, perhaps: that autonomy of language is
     also their cultural heritage; that is, the uses to which their
     shared language has been put by successive past generations of
     members of their culture, and as whose senses it may still be
     available. Schutz characterizes language's everyday vernaculars
     as treasure-houses of pre-constituted types (words), each carry-
     ing along an open horizon of meaning (1962, p.14). The pre-
     constitutions record uses of vernacular words by past gener-
     ations of members of cultures, and their senses fill words'
     horizons of meaning with bewildering arrays of alternatives.
     Dilemmas of present members are in limiting those horizons by
     reducing each array of alternatives to a 'meaningful' few. To
     recognition of this social task sensibility is crucial; and to
     its solution it is indispensable.

22   It is axiomatic for Leavis that students able to benefit from a
     university education (as he proposes it) can never be more than
     a minority of any social group of young adults. See, especially
     on this (1948) and (1969).

23   The passages that follow are quoted to show Leavis's view of
     modern English society to be essentially conservative in a sense
     that depends on my reading of David Caute's remarks on differ-
     ences between left- and right-wing ideologies in relation to
     socio-politically committed literature (Caute, 1971, pp.53-5 and
     passim). There is no simple coincidence of relevances between
     Caute's and Leavis's work here, however. The view of art that
     Caute castigates by his invocation of the implicit character of
     conservative ideologies within it is not that of Leavis, to whom
     Caute's castigations (as opposed to his remarks on conservative
     ideology) are not at all relevant. Raymond Williams has made,
     it seems to me, an explicit mistake of this kind, from a radi-
     cal, socio-politically committed position (see Williams, 1958,
     pp.246-57).

24   To do so, though, is to appear to depart from Leavis's pro-
     posals, for upon 'those admonitory hints one has heard that, to
     be taken seriously, university English, besides affording a
     lodgement to linguistic science, must aspire to be a social
     science itself'; he comments further that 'it would be better
     for us all if they (i.e. 'social studies') were pursued and
     studied, in so far as they aspire to be authoritative sources of
     knowledge and wisdom about human nature and human life, in the
     climate, intellectual and spiritual, that a due performance of
     the function would generate' (1969, p.173). I would claim that
     this is not such a departure, however. What I shall propose
     would be, if implemented, unavoidably of that climate.

25   Almost invariably not: sociologists appear to claim authorship

for their work more often individually than socially (déspite acknowledgments to others - which are invariably, anyway, qualified into nullity by individual personal disclaimers). This paper is no exception.

26 The question may be formulated, in a way more directly relevant to issues implicit in foregoing sections of this paper, as: what are the differences between professional sociologies and Leavis's, or a Leavisite, or a Leavis-like version of literary criticism?

27 On 'uninteresting, essential' reflexivities as constitutive, problematic phenomena of sociologies, see Garfinkel (1967, pp.7-9 and passim).

28 Considered here as a version of epistemological continuity in comparatively recent Western social thought, exegetically organized as interrelated searches by a number of thinkers for the character of what is understood as the social through its scholarly and imaginative study. See, for example, Parsons (1937, p.99); Nisbet (1966); Zeitlin (1967).

29 See, for example, Durkheim (1938); Weber (1949); Schutz (1962).

30 This is not to hold that the practices of scientific investigation are not widely (if not universally) established and held logical practices. It is, though, to recommend that they be considered as established and held socially, by the social community of professional scientists whose mutually recognized social practices are science; and that their logic is the socio-logic produced by the members of that community as criteria for the mutual recognition of their practices. (See David Walsh's paper, 'Science, Sociology and Everyday Life', in this volume.)

BIBLIOGRAPHY

Throughout this bibliography, all dates in brackets are those of first publication of the works to which they refer. Dates not enclosed in brackets are those of other editions consulted to which references are made in the text of the paper.

ANNAN, Lord (1966), 'The Disintegration of an Old Culture', Oxford, Clarendon Press.
ANNAN, Lord (1970), The University and the Intellect: Miasma and the Menace, 'The Times Literary Supplement', 30 April.
BANTOCK, G.H. (1963), 'Education in an Industrial Society', Faber.
BELL, D. (1960), 'The End of Ideology', Chicago, Free Press. New York, Collier Books, 1962.
BERGER, P. and BERGER, B. (1970), 'Sociology', Garden City, N.Y., Doubleday.
BENSMAN, J. and VIDICH, A.L. (1958), 'Small Town in Mass Society', Princeton University Press. Garden City, N.Y., Anchor Books, 1960.
BENTLEY, E. (ed.) (1948), 'The Importance of "Scrutiny"'. New York University Press, 1964.
BRAMSON, L. (1960), The Political Context of Sociology, Princeton University Press.

BOURNE, G. (1912), 'Change in the Village', Duckworth.

BOURNE, G. (1923), 'The Wheelwright's Shop', New York, Cambridge University Press.

CAUTE, D. (1971), 'The Illusion'. Panther, 1972.

CICOUREL, A.V. (1973), 'Cognitive Sociology', Penguin.

DURKHEIM, E. (1938), 'The Rules of Sociological Method', University of Chicago Press.

ELIOT, T.S. (1920), 'The Sacred Wood: Essays in Poetry and Criticism'. Methuen, 1928.

FILMER, P. (1969), The Literary Imagination and the Explanation of Socio-Cultural Change in Modern Britain, 'European Journal of Sociology', vol.X.

FOWLES, J. (1964), 'The Aristos'. Toronto, New American Library of Canada, 1970.

GARFINKEL, H. (1967), 'Studies in Ethnomethodology', Englewood Cliffs, N.J., Prentice-Hall.

KORNHAUSER, W. (1960), 'The Politics of Mass Society', Routledge & Kegan Paul.

LEAVIS, F.R. (1932), The Literary Mind, 'Scrutiny', vol.I, no.1.

LEAVIS, F.R. (1934), Under Which King, Bezonian? 'Scrutiny', vol.I, no.3.

LEAVIS, F.R. (1943), 'Education and the University'. Chatto & Windus, 1948.

LEAVIS, F.R. (1950), Introduction to 'Mill on Bentham and Coleridge', Chatto & Windus.

LEAVIS, F.R. (1952a), 'The Great Tradition', Chatto & Windus.

LEAVIS, F.R. (1952b), 'The Common Pursuit', Chatto & Windus. Penguin, 1966.

LEAVIS, F.R. (1955), 'D.H.Lawrence: Novelist'. Penguin, 1964.

LEAVIS, F.R. (1969), 'English Literature in our Time and the University', Chatto & Windus.

LEAVIS, F.R. (1972), 'Nor Shall My Sword: Discourses on Pluralism, Compassion and Social Hope', Chatto & Windus.

LEAVIS, F.R. and LEAVIS, Q.D. (1970), 'Dickens, the Novelist', Penguin.

LEAVIS, F.R. and THOMPSON, D. (1933), 'Culture and Environment', Chatto & Windus.

LYND, R.S. and LYND, H.M. (1956), 'Middletown', New York, Harcourt, Brace.

McQUAIL, D. (1969), 'Towards a Sociology of Mass Communications', Collier-Macmillan.

MARCUS, S. (1972), The Mystery of Pickwick, 'Daedalus', Winter.

NISBET, R. (1966), 'The Sociological Tradition', New York, Basic Books.

PARSONS, T. (1937), 'The Structure of Social Action', New York, Free Press.

RICKWOOD, E. (1933), T.S.Eliot: 'Selected Essays' - A Review, 'Scrutiny', vol.I, no.4.

ROSENBERG, B. and WHITE, D.M. (1958), 'Mass Culture: the Popular Arts in America', Chicago, Free Press.

ROSENBERG, B. and WHITE, D.M. (1970), 'Mass Culture Revisited', New York, Van Nostrand.

SANDYWELL, B. et al. (1975), 'Problems of Reflexitivity and Dialectics in Sociological Inquiry: Language Theorising Difference', Routledge & Kegan Paul.

SCHUTZ, A. (1962), 'Collected Papers', vol.I, The Hague, Martinus Nijhoff.
SNOW, C.P. (1969), 'The Two Cultures and A Second Look', Cambridge University Press.
SNOW, C.P. (1970), The Case of Leavis and the Serious Case, 'The Times Literary Supplement', 9 July.
THOMPSON, D. (1964), 'Discrimination and Popular Culture', Penguin.
WEBER, M. (1949), 'The Methodology of the Social Sciences', New York, Free Press.
WILLIAMS, R. (1958), 'Culture and Society, 1780-1950', Chatto & Windus. Penguin, 1964.
WILLIAMS, R. (1961), 'The Long Revolution', Chatto & Windus.
WILLIAMS, R. (1973), 'The Country and the City', Chatto & Windus.
ZEITLIN, I. (1967), 'Ideology and the Development of Sociological Theory', Englewood Cliffs, N.J., Prentice-Hall.

Chapter 6

TAKING SIDES AGAINST THE PROBABLE
Problems of relativity
and commitment in teaching
and the sociology of knowledge

Michael F.D.Young

The occasion of this paper is to focus several concerns of the
writer, and an opportunity therefore to work them through publicly,
albeit in a tentative and often inchoate form. The first issue
arises out of the increasing relevance for redefining the problems
that many of us working in the sociology of education have found in
what for the moment I shall refer to as 'the sociology of
knowledge'. The enthusiasm with which I certainly have accepted
this redefinition has perhaps allowed the problem of relativism to
be too readily dismissed (often as 'just the philosophers'
problem'). The second concern is with teachers, who can read this
relativism, and in fact much sociological inquiry in education (as
it becomes free from the isolating of children's 'background' attributes as determining educational achievement), as not so much redefining problems but 'undermining action' - their action, as
teachers. These issues lead finally to reconsidering the relationship between sociological inquiry and the practice of teaching.
This is taken up in the last section through a reading of Merleau-
Ponty. What I want to suggest is that, far from leading to the
despair often associated with relativism, a sociology of knowledge,
or, as it seems better to call it, a reflexive sociology (see
O'Neill, 1972), in recognizing that the grounds of its commitment
are those of our common humanity, points to the possibility of
collaboration which transcends institutional categories such as
research and teaching. To the extent that this commitment is, in
whatever social or historical context, to an idea of human liber-
ation, this, as I see it, suggests following through, with those
involved, the alternatives that inquiry might point to. The paper,
therefore is divided into five sections:
1 Conceptions of the sociology of knowledge;
2 Sociologists' and teachers' predicaments;
3 'Knowledge as truth criteria' or 'knowledge as power'?
4 Merleau-Ponty and the contingency of social life;
5 What's it to do with us?

CONCEPTIONS OF THE SOCIOLOGY OF KNOWLEDGE

It is possible to view a term or a category like the sociology of knowledge as having two very distinct kinds of meaning which would generate very different kinds of 'problem'. Since Mannheim and Scheler, particularly in the USA, it has been seen as a fairly distinct body of writing concerned with the social character of knowledge; within this body of writing several loosely conceived traditions can be discerned. They can be distinguished, broadly, by how they characterize 'social', 'knowledge', and the implications of viewing knowledge as social. Often it has been later interpreters who have incorporated earlier writings into their new category, 'the sociology of knowledge' – we nowhere find the term in the work of Marx or Schutz, who was late enough in time to refer to a 'so-called sociology of knowledge'. I shall make brief reference to rather than review what are commonly labelled perspectives or approaches in the sociology of knowledge, and the kind of inquiries into education they either have given rise to or have been called on to legitimate. The 'body of knowledge' notion of a sociology of knowledge, which such a review implies, is unsatisfactory in many respects that I have not the space to elaborate on here. The unexamined assumptions that there are implications for the sociology of education, and that what emerges will be significant for educational practice, beg just the questions that we need to raise. In failing to treat the sociology of knowledge as social, such sociology fails to be reflexive about the grounds of its own activity. The emergence and sustenance by practitioners in their own writing, teaching and research of categories such as 'sociology of knowledge' and 'sociological theory', which have implications, relevance, etc. for a sociology of education, would seem an important topic for a history of ideas, which I shall not try to deal with. Phrases like 'implications for' and 'relevance of' in this context suggest assumptions about the character of the sociology of education as a form of inquiry; in particular that such an inquiry is atheoretical, and does not operate even implicitly with notions about the social grounds of all knowledge. Both seem to have unfortunate consequences, one of which is the hiving off of 'curriculum' or 'knowledge' as a topic in the sociology of education. Thus 'curriculum' is perpetuated, as Maxine Greene (1971) puts it, as 'a structure of socially prescribed knowledge ... external to the knower, there to be ... mastered, learned' rather than 'a possibility for him [the learner] as an existing person, mainly concerned with making sense of his own life world'.

There are important issues that I shall only be peripherally concerned with, such as the on-going debates about the inadequacies of Durkheimian, Marxist and phenomenological perspectives. Durkheim is challenged for being concerned with the 'reproduction' rather than the production of knowledge; phenomenologists for an emphasis on how knowledge is constructed, how the world is made real, rather than why it is made real in particular ways; and Marx for an ambiguity over the status of science and technology. One reason for avoiding such debates is that they depend on holistic and reified notions of the writer or perspective under discussion; depending on how one reads a work, demonstrations of inadequacies are always possible. A different and to me more fruitful view is to see a sociology of knowledge as not distinct from a sociology, in the sense that all sociology is a sociology of knowledge. The notions of everyday, commonsense or tacit knowledge, the knowledge that we draw on whatever we are doing, are not then viewed as distinct from the formalized bodies of knowledge such as philosophy, science and literature. In operating even implicitly with such a distinction, as say Berger and Luckmann (1966) appear to, unavoidably one takes over the view that religion, philosophy etc. are the thought systems produced by small groups of 'experts', and thus the nature of the thinking of the rest of humanity is different and, to the extent that it is non-philosophical, non-scientific etc., known.

If then the sociology of knowledge becomes taking a theoretical stance to the character of social life - whether it is setting essays, marking exam scripts or whatever, there will be no necessary implications, relevance, etc. except in so far as those involved in such activities perceive them. This would suggest a rather differ-ent kind of question which emerges as much from a reflexive view of teaching as from a reflexive sociology. (The link between this notion of reflexivity and a conception of commitment which is raised later is explored in Keddie and Young (1972).) For instance, how do teachers discover and use what they 'know' in the day-to-day situ-ations of the classroom? This kind of question can be illustrated by referring to a familiar discrepancy between 'academic' and 'teacher' perspectives, represented hypothetically here:

A.   'My ideas are always oversimplified and misunderstood.'
T.   'Even if I had the time, I cannot understand the language.'

In the light of what has been said, these comments could be in-terpreted as follows. If we recognize the 'contextual' or 'situ-ational' character of what we know, then an idea, finding etc. will have quite different relevance for different users - in this case academic and teacher. One might well go on to ask then, why are teachers, typically, so uninterested in treating their own activi-ties critically? And, equally, why are most writers on education (but not only education), more concerned with communicating to other 'so called' theorists than with the practitioners about whom they claim to theorize about?

SOCIOLOGISTS' AND TEACHERS' PREDICAMENTS

The issue then is, first, the predicament of the sociologist who takes the social character of his as well as all other knowledge, seriously. Such a position appears to argue for a total relativism, and the destructive nihilism that is its possible conclusion. The only possible alternative that follows from a rejection of this relativism appears to be to ground one's critique of relativism in an epistemological position that makes it 'philosophically untena-ble'.

It is a paradox that, while the 'radical doubt' of relativism has posed the most challenging questions of recent sociology, this 'doubt' is a 'theoretical' and not a 'practical' possibility, whether the practice is 'doing sociology', teaching or anything else. More specifically, what I mean here is that, as one can only retro-

spectively, and even then partially, provide for the grounds of any
action, it may be that the notion of reflexivity, whether in relation to sociology or teaching, is then necessarily collaborative
or in other words involves others. This may be the same dilemma
that arises from a commitment to call into question 'members' categories' (in Garfinkel's sense) that at the same time we find ourselves using - education and ability are just two of many examples.
It is possible therefore that the 'crutches' offered by 'objectivist' theories of knowledge may be seen as an attempt to evade
something fundamental like being a person, historically and socially
situated, and as such, oneself, responsible.

Parallel to the predicament just outlined is that of the teacher,
or other practitioner, confronted with a sociological account that
calls into question the grounds of his or her activities. Such an
account is one thing in an on-going debate between groups of sociologists with different perspectives, but quite another for the
teacher in a context where these grounds are part of what he shares
with other teachers and which make his own activities possible.
This predicament might be made more explicit (and not just, though
certainly quite plausibly, as a teacher's defence mechanism) by
conceiving of the imaginary teacher calling into question the
grounds of the practice of university or college sociologists. But
let us elaborate on this with some typical examples from what has,
in a recent article, been called 'the new sociology of education'
(Gorbutt, 1972). This starts by rejecting the assumption of any
superiority of educational or 'academic' knowledge over the everyday
commonsense knowledge available to people as being in the world.
There is no doubt that teachers' practices - lecturing, syllabus
construction, examining, writing textbooks, etc. - are predicated on
just the assumption of the superiority of academic knowledge that is
being called into question. Practical recognition of this is to be
found in the 'educational arguments for raising the school-leaving
age, and the academic credentials demanded as 'necessary' by those
selecting people for various kinds of work. Nowhere is this discrepancy between the assumptions of educators and of sociologists
more apparent than in the accounts sociologists and teachers give
of school failure. Whereas teachers 'know' that some children are
'less able', 'not trying', 'come from bad homes' etc., sociological
accounts suggest that such knowledge generates from 'hierarchical
notions of ability', 'pathological views of working class family
life', and an identification of minority class culture as 'the
culture' of which such children are deprived. (1) The point at
issue is the significance of this discrepancy. To the extent that
sociologists (and others) view their activity as in some way helping
the student - or practising teacher - these accounts will be seen as
undermining and in a real sense 'not relevant'. However, I would
suggest that this is to misconceive the sociological enterprise in
two ways: first, though calling into question the superiority of
'academic knowledge' - the sociologist is not raising the same
question about sociological knowledge, and second in that the lesson
of Marx's eleventh Thesis on Feuerbach (translation 1970) has not
been learnt. 'Philosophers [and here read sociologists] have only
interpreted the world ... the point is to change it', and as Alan
Blum (1971) puts it, 'theorizing [or sociology or philosophy] is

not designed to save worlds ... It is ordinary men who try to save worlds ... through their ordinary practical notions, sometimes aided by theories, but usually in spite of them.' However, though Marx and Blum point to change as a practical activity, Marx in particular is reminding us that a theory has significance only in so far as it is lived through in a course of action; and as his own life exemplified, sociologists, philosophers and teachers are ordinary men and women as well and, more importantly, first.

To return to an earlier point, if, as was suggested earlier, relativism is a practical impossibility in sociological inquiry or anything else, it may be that certain familiar distinctions are oversimplified. I am thinking for example of those who find the notions of 'relativizing' and 'radical doubt' challenging and exciting, and those who reject such notions and rush to the security of various kinds of epistemology, vulgar Marxism, notions of 'structure' or perhaps the belief that radical doubt is an academic luxury that involves a denial of moral and political concern. If the former at some point implicitly have to reject their own radical doubt, because all doubt is from a starting point, then they too make reference to some criteria or grounds, however uncertain. The difference may only be that, whereas for the former this uncertainty is recognized as part of the fate of being human, for the latter it is a kind of terror where everything seems in danger of collapsing.

In trying not to resolve but confront the meaning of these issues in teaching and sociology, I turn to what I call versions of 'the philosophical escape'.

'KNOWLEDGE AS TRUTH CRITERIA' OR 'KNOWLEDGE AS POWER'?

I start from Wright Mills's (1940) sociological critique of knowledge. He argues that logics, truth criteria and rules of proof are, like all we know, grounded in common cultures rather than anything external to those who use such rules. Thus what is logical is a question of how in a particular context a particular rule is used. Rules, then, are viewed as members' categories, and members call on others' knowledge of a common culture of logic, which provides them with normative criteria in terms of which they can give meaning to statements about logicality and identify the illogical, the non-logical, the false, the probable and the true. To put it another way, logic is far from being abstract, but totally relativized, to the situation of its use. Mills tackles the argument that in undermining its own position such a view of knowledge is self-contradictory, by saying that this only holds if one already starts with external criteria of truth. However there are problems in Mills's analysis and Dewey's pragmatic logic that he draws on, which are raised in a paper by Rytina and Loomis (1970), though they for quite other reasons deal with Dewey and Marx, and in fact use Mills's critique of pragmatism for support. In accepting, as pragmatic and dialectical theories of knowledge do, that truth criteria are 'developing things', not external to the inquiry or the practice, Rytina and Loomis argue that these are, in effect, no criteria at all; Marx, Dewey and by implication Mills, they claim, operate with what they call 'activist criteria of truth'. Such criteria, in

relying on the method of inquiry, without 'external' checks, depend
inevitably on those who use them. The guarantee for Dewey is a
naive faith in the toleration of open-ended inquiry, and in an opti-
mism that this will lead to progress towards the 'good society'.
Such a toleration of inquiry neither was nor is a characteristic of
American or any other society, thus opening the way, as Rytina and
Loomis see it, to a situation, as in the Soviet Union, where those
who have power define the truth.

Whatever the crudities of Rytina and Loomis's account of Marxist
theory, they raise serious issues for a sociological conception of
knowledge as exemplified in 'Knowledge and Control' (Young, 1971),
at any rate in the introduction, which relies very much on Mills.
The implications of treating what counts as knowledge as problematic
is inevitably to abandon notions of formal logic and to offer no
explicit epistemology or truth criteria. The question quite plausibly becomes, What status and validity (if any) can one give to the
results of such a project? (2)

It is understandable therefore that some kind of alternative to
what might be characterized as a combination of naive idealism,
extreme relativism and throughgoing pragmatism that can be readily
seen as resulting in a solipsistic view that makes no sense of sociology or any other kind of inquiry. In exploring the issues raised,
I do not see this as an academic argument in the normal sense of the
term, but as offering the grounds of a project that does not divorce
sociological inquiry from political action. (I use political in
Paulo Freire's sense that all action is political (Freire, 1972a and
b).)

Early on in their paper Rytina and Loomis make the point that
'the methods prescribed [by Marx and Dewey] have an important
defect, in that they permit although they do not require those in
power to define truth'; the assumption must be that other methods
(presumably versions of formal logic) neither permit nor require
such a possibility. To conceive of the possibility of such methods
is necessarily to conceive of remedying the indexicality of rules,
of reconstructing rules of logic that are also logics-in-use; rules
that in some way do not need interpreting as applicable in any particular situation. Contrary to this I would argue that all methods,
pragmatic, Marxist, scientific, formal or whatever, have just this
'defect', if such it is to be called, that is irremediable – that
they have to be 'used', and only take on their meaning in the
context of their use. This then is not so much a defect of certain
methods, but a claim to deny, on behalf of some formal systems, the
fundamental contingency of their use. The merit of the Rytina and
Loomis paper is that, in considering Marx and Dewey, they take two
notions of truth that explicitly do not try to claim their version
of truth as grounded in logic or science (though some versions of
Marxism do). Truth for Dewey is grounded in 'rational enquiring
man', and for Marx in the unique humanity of the proletariat, though
the significance of this is blurred by Rytina and Loomis through
their propaganda-like characterization of 'goodness to fit' models
for pragmatism and American society and Marxism and Soviet society,
and a naively mechanicistic view of power determining knowledge as
exemplified in the 'Lysencko affair'.

However, it is my contention that the problems of validity of

truth criteria or relativism in the sociology of knowledge are still
evaded rather than confronted, whether one turns to one of a váriety
of objectivistic views of knowledge, to Dewey's 'rational man'
(which has the same kind of limited historical specificity that
Marcuse demonstrated in Weber's 'rational actor') or to Marx's
proletariat, 'the one class capable of recognizing one another and
therefore of founding humanity', as Merleau-Ponty puts it.

MERLEAU-PONTY AND THE CONTINGENCY OF SOCIAL LIFE

In 'Humanism and Terror' (1969) Merleau-Ponty is concerned to try
and understand, not to judge, the Stalinist purges in Russia in the
1930s. I want to suggest that he may provide a way of looking at
the issues raised in this paper that recognizes them as experienced;
that does not treat such an activity as an academic exercise, but as
an acknowledgment of the contingency and openness of history. 'What
happens is never inevitable, but is made to happen' - a statement as
true of Lenin and Trotsky (who, though they had 'theories of revolution', still had to make it themselves) as of anyone else. In
this early study Merleau-Ponty seems to face the contradiction involved in the search for certainty in an uncertain world where, as
he puts it, 'we have to work without certainty in confusion towards
truth'. I see this as the human dilemma that was presented as so-
called epistemological argument in the previous section. It must
also be a critical question for both sociologists and teachers, who
are I take it concerned both to understand the social world as a
world of human beings and at the same time to treat those we seek to
teach or understand as themselves human. In dismissing Koestler's
moral abhorrence of the purges, their portrayal as 'justice' by the
Soviet state, and as 'necessary' by the French communists, Merleau-
Ponty argues that each limits us from understanding what it was to
be human in a particular historical context. Such a conception appears to me as the beginning of a way beyond the destructive nihilism that the relativism of the sociology of knowledge can imply, as
well as an avoidance of the dependency on external criteria that
appears to remove responsibility from the person, whether teacher or
researcher. The next section will not try to summarize the book,
but rather raise the issues that seem relevant to the previous part
of this paper; its themes come alive much more in the characters of
Stalin, Bukharin and Trotsky and their interpreters Koestler and the
author than they can in my brief comments.
  The violence and uncertainty that for Merleau-Ponty underlie the
fragile stability and order of our lives become apparent only in
times of conquest and revolution - when the French state collapsed
in 1940, all notions of hierarchy, legitimacy and legality, which
had been taken as given, collapsed too. In this kind of situation
people cannot avoid choosing, and taking the consequences of their
choice, in a future they cannot even think they know; such are the
fundamental characteristics of history and social life all the time,
though it is usually possible to live as if they were not. Men are
seen as normally justifying their actions with claims to know their
likely consequences; to do so they call on criteria of rationality,
morality and necessity, and the whole range of theories, laws and

sciences. It is questionable then whether the sciences of man, such
as sociology, do little more than confirm these 'believed' necessi-
ties, thus helping to avoid what are for Merleau-Ponty the specifically human elements of human life - its contingency, its risks, its
involvement with others and, as is the concern of most of his work,
the primacy of our own perception of the world. The risks and contingency alluded to stem from a recognition of how the perceptions
in terms of which we act are inevitably partial and limited socially
and historically. However in a curious way which takes us back to
the earlier discussion, in being the only grounds for action we
have, these perceptions are also, for the person, absolute. In
these terms the relativism of any human grounds becomes an absolute,
not an absolute of certainty provided by some external agency or
rule system, nor a solipsistic absolute which implies a 'can-do-
anything' nihilism, but an absolute that implies a recognition that
whatever one does involves commitment, risk of failure and disil-
lusion, whatever our intentions.

Events, for Merleau-Ponty, are how they are interpreted - this is
not the naive idealism it may appear, because with no science of the
future they may always be different, and with no destiny a future
may be believed in with a theory like Marxism, but this can never
remove the inevitability of choice, to make that future happen, when
confronted with the unknown exigencies of others. No situation,
then, not even physical violence, is absolutely compelling, in the
sense that the compulsion is not perceived; thus the sciences,
logics and ethics, may be guides, but the action, whether in
research, teaching or whatever, is a decision - not a private decision, but a public or political one - to 'insert ourselves in a
course of events'. Such distinctions, so favoured by liberal philosophers as circumstances and will, intention and action, object
and subject, are, Merleau-Ponty argues, merely super-impositions on
the experience of 'having to act when we don't know what we are
doing' - when the future is always uncertain, and when the conflict
between consistently acting within our worth as we experience it and
not wanting to disavow what we are to others is always with us.
Commitment, choice, responsibility, contingency, future unknown and
future to be made - these are some of the words and phrases that
echo through 'Humanism and Terror', from a Marxist who realized that
a Marxist theory even for Marx was not enough, and from a phenome-
nologist who recognized than what men perceived, though all for
them, but was far from all in terms of history or social life.

It is possible, though inevitably oversimplifying, to extract
three specific points that sum up this brief account and refer directly to the issues raised earlier in this paper. First, there is
the rejection of the crutches of bourgeois or Marxist scientism, or
any kind of external logics or moralities; not for themselves, but
as ways of avoiding specifically human and personal commitments.
Second, there is the explicit recognition that all acting is 'acting
at risk', and therefore of the 'bad faith' of the academic spectator
in mental isolation reviewing others' commitments, or as he puts it
'the peculiar intellectual prejudice of trotting through perspectives without setting on one, thereby understanding everything
but that others too have perspectives'. Third, his description of
the French resistance fighters as 'taking sides against the proba-

ble' suggests a direct challenge to much of our social life which is concerned with 'living with the probable' and to much of our social science, concerned as it is with discovering the probable.

WHAT'S IT TO DO WITH US?

This paper may appear to have taken us far from the original concerns about teaching and the sociology of knowledge. I don't think so, however, and I want to finish by tentatively suggesting some of the reasons why. If we recognize the absolute character of anyone's actions, however partial and relative the knowledge one has, then it would appear that the problematics of the sociology of knowledge are not distinct, except as institutional artefacts of the academy, from the problematics of social life. In other words, the epistemological problems raised earlier are fundamentally human ones; for, to the extent that one recognizes that we are unavoidably committed as persons, such a recognition, though with all the risks of being a person that are expressed in fears of nihilism, also involves all the possibilities, expressed in the title of this paper, of 'taking sides against the probable'. Though Merleau-Ponty's book addresses itself to 'political man', whose fate it is to 'do nothing or be criminal', no less is it addressed to the sociologist, the teacher or the researcher, for each of whom 'action is impure', and groundless in the sense that the rules of logic, science or morality may be guides, but are never grounds. By depending on or searching for external criteria outside of what we do, we avoid the experiential truth of still having to choose, of unavoidably being 'engaged with others in a common history'. It is this last point that leaves the discussion open, not closed; for each of us has to discover what, at a particular time, it means to be human and what 'is probable'. Some of the confusion and quite justifiable antagonism felt by practitioners such as teachers towards sociologists might be removed if both realized that they share a common human history, and that often categories such as 'teacher' and 'sociologist', while appearing to protect them as persons, in effect often prevent the possibility of their so being. At the very least, this possibility involves us in recognizing our responsibility to follow through with those whose accounts we call into question the alternatives that this questioning suggests. How we do this, or what the implications might be for research for anyone concerned as a sociologist with the work of teachers, it seems important to leave as I suggested above, as something that only each of us can discover for ourselves. (3) This follows from the main argument of this paper, that it is in the end personal commitments that are the grounds for action, whether that action is deciding what to do in the classroom or the 'adequacy' of a researcher's account. The point then is not to ask whether particular research methods are, of themselves, 'good' or 'bad', but to ask for what and for whom are we providing accounts.

ACKNOWLEDGMENTS

This paper originally appeared in 'Educational Review', vol.25
(1973) and is reproduced by permission.
    Many friends have read and commented on an earlier draft of this
paper, among whom I would particularly like to thank John
Bartholomew, John Beck, Nell Keddie, Charles Posner, David Walsh and
Geoff Whitty. I have certainly not yet been able to do justice to
the points they raised, but I owe more to their encouragement and
support in that very isolated activity of writing than can be expressed in the usual rituals of acknowledgments.

NOTES

1 These ideas are discussed by Keddie (1971) in her work as con-
   sultant for the Open University, and in her more recent work
   (1973), each of which has extensive bibliographies.
2 These questions were first raised in conversation with John Hayes
   of King's College, London, and also in further discussion with
   John Beck of Homerton College, Cambridge. Neither, of course,
   are in any way responsible for my particular formulation of what
   I learnt from them.
3 Bartholomew in a recent paper (1972) has made some important suggestions.

BIBLIOGRAPHY

BARTHOLOMEW, J.C. (1972), Teachers as Researchers - paper presented
to the York Conference, Social Deprivation and Educational Change.
BERGER, P. and LUCKMANN, T.P. (1966), 'The Social Construction of
Reality', Penguin.
BLUM, A. (1971), Methods of Recognizing, Describing and Formulating
Social Problems, in O.Smigel (ed.), 'Handbook on the Study of Social
Problems', Chicago, Rand McNally.
FREIRE, P. (1972a), 'Cultural Action for Freedom', Penguin.
FREIRE, P. (1972b), 'Pedagogy of the Oppressed', Penguin.
GORBUTT, D.A. (1972), The New Sociology of Education, 'Education for
Teaching', November.
GREENE, M. (1971), Curriculum and Consciousness, 'Record', vol.73,
no.2.
KEDDIE, N. (1971), Classroom Knowledge, in M.F.D.Young (1971),
'Knowledge and Control: New Directions for the Sociology of Edu-
cation', Collier-Macmillan.
KEDDIE, N. (ed.) (1973), 'Tinker, Tailor ... The Myth of Cultural
Deprivation', Penguin.
KEDDIE, N. and YOUNG, M.F.D. (1972), New Directions: Is Anything
Happening in Sociology? (unpublished mimeograph).
MARX, K. (translation 1970), Thesis on Feuerbach, in K.Marx and
F.Engels, 'The German Ideology', Lawrence & Wishart.
MARX, K. and ENGELS, F. (1970), 'The German Ideology', Lawrence &
Wishart.
MERLEAU-PONTY, M. (1969), 'Humanism and Terror', New York, Beacon
Books.

MILLS, C.Wright (1940), The Methodological Consequences of the
Sociology of Knowledge, 'American Journal of Sociology', vol.XLVI,
no.3.
O'NEILL, J. (1972), 'Sociology as a Skin Trade', Heinemann.
RYTINA, J.H. and LOOMIS, C.P. (1970), Marxist Dialectic and Pragmatism: Power as Knowledge, 'American Sociological Review', vol.35,
no.2.
YOUNG, M.F.D. (ed.) (1971), 'Knowledge and Control: New Directions
for the Sociology of Education', Collier-Macmillan.